INTRODUCTION TO
MUSICAL KNOWLEDGE

UNIVERSITY OF MINNESOTA BAND, GERALD R. PRESCOTT, DIRECTOR

ST. OLAF CHOIR, DR. F. MELIUS CHRISTIANSEN, DIRECTOR

INTRODUCTION TO MUSICAL KNOWLEDGE

by

ARCHIE N. JONES
UNIVERSITY OF MINNESOTA

and

FLOYD P. BARNARD
ROOSEVELT HIGH SCHOOL, MINNEAPOLIS

Paul A. Schmitt Music Company
MINNEAPOLIS

First Printing, September, 1935
Second Printing, January, 1936
Third Printing, September, 1936
Fourth Printing, August, 1937
Fifth Printing, June, 1938
Sixth Printing, October, 1938

Gratefully
inscribed to the students of the
University High School

FOREWORD

THROUGH experiences acquired in the teaching of music in high schools, the authors have sensed a need for a brief, concise text covering the "tool" subjects in music: theory, harmony, history, and form. The present volume is an attempt to meet that need. No effort has been made to cover any of the subjects exhaustively. Rather, the book aims to orient the student to the whole subject of music, to give a clear picture of the language of music, and to present some rudimentary lessons in the understanding of musical elements.

While music appreciation has not been specifically mentioned, it is the underlying purpose of the book. The authors believe that any degree of appreciation beyond a mere sense appreciation must depend upon a foundation of musical information, and that the degree of appreciation increases proportionately with an increase in musical knowledge. Appreciation has been described as a sort of complex attitude toward music, which includes not only an understanding of music itself, and a knowledge of the processes involved in its composition and performance, but an emotional attitude as well. The authors have therefore set forth in this volume some of the factual information necessary to an understanding of our musical system, with the hope that it will contribute to a better appreciation of music.

It is to be hoped that frequent reference will be made to the glossary of musical terms. It is composed not only of the terms used in the book, but includes in addition most of the musical terms in common use, derived from a study by the authors of over six million running words in newspaper and magazine reading. The composers whose biographies are given in Chapter VI are those whose works appeared most frequently in more than five hundred concert programs examined. The authors consider therefore, that this list might well be the basis for intensive study.

TABLE OF CONTENTS

ILLUSTRATIONS

CHAPTER I

MUSICAL THEORY

" . . . All the king's horses and all the king's men,
Couldn't put Humpty together again."

IF WE were to take all the notes of Beethoven's Fifth Symphony apart and scramble them together in a large box, no one, not even Beethoven, could reconstruct them in such a fashion that the result would be the Fifth Symphony again, *unless* he remembered every melody, every harmony, and every rhythm as it occurred the first time. What, then, is the secret of being able to place the elements of music,—melody, rhythm, and harmony—together in such a fashion that they make a unified and meaningful whole? The answer, of course, is obvious: a thorough knowledge of these elements, plus the ability to create through them a composition that carries a message to the listeners. Anyone can acquire the knowledge; only a Beethoven can possess the ability to weld the elements into a Fifth Symphony. Knowledge of the elements constitutes the essentials of musical theory, and it is with the latter that our first chapter is concerned.

Each one of the professions or vocations has its own vocabulary. If we converse with a group of lawyers, we talk in terms of "torts," "contracts" and "statutes;" if we talk with artists, we speak of "pigments" "hues" and "values." It is not necessary, of course, that everyone learn all the words used in all divisions of knowledge. If we wish to appreciate and understand the world about us, however, we must learn enough of the vocabularies of the other people to give us an insight into their problems, accomplishments, and knowledge. Thus, if we wish to appreciate music, we must learn a small portion of the vocabulary of music. (It is to be hoped that the glossary of musical terms will be used often for reference.) The number of words we possess and can use correctly is an index of our general knowledge. Likewise, the more musical terms we know and can use, the better we can understand the music of everyday life.

Musical theory, however, is something more than mere vocabulary. It includes not only the names of things, but the *uses* of things as well. One well versed in theory should have no trouble in writing a song. Of course that song might not possess any musical value; it might lack the spark of genius. Nevertheless, one who possesses the necessary knowledge to put music together, possesses the knowledge to take it apart, or analyze it, and it is through this process that the highest degree of appreciation comes. Let us proceed, then, to the discussion of some of the more common elements of music.

MUSICAL NOTATION

The *staff* is a series of five horizontal lines. Upon these lines and in the spaces between them are placed the notes of the scale. The use of the staff dates back to about 900 A.D. when a staff of only one line was used. Above and below this line, which represented a certain pitch, were placed peculiar marks called "neumes" to indicate the rise and fall of the melody. From this primitive staff, the development was slow and gradual. Various numbers of lines were used from time to time, as many as fifteen having been used in one musical system. Sometimes the lines only were used, and at others both the lines and spaces. Finally, about 1500 A.D. our present five line staff was invented, and both the lines and spaces were used to designate successive steps in the scale system.

The staff may be extended to include more notes by adding short lines above or below the staff. These are called "leger lines." Notes may be placed on either the lines or in the spaces above or below. The "great staff" is the term used when the treble and bass staffs are combined, as in music for the piano or organ.

GREAT STAFF

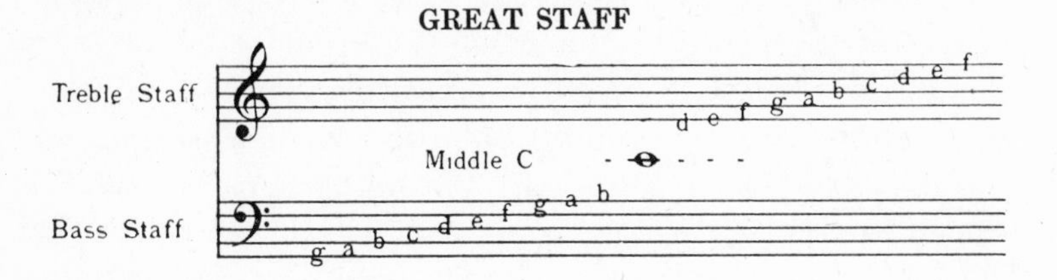

The "clef" is a sign placed at the beginning of the staff to show the pitches to be represented by the lines and spaces. The clef is necessary because of the tremendous range in pitch from the lowest instrument or voice to the highest. Each instrument is capable of playing only in a certain range of pitch. It would be obviously impossible to place on one staff, even if leger lines were used, all the notes played by all the instruments. Therefore, in writing music, it is necessary to use different clefs for different instruments and voices.

Before describing each clef, it will be necessary to explain briefly the physical background of tone. Sound is caused by motion or vibration. Musical tone is the result of regular, or evenly-spaced vibration. The difference in pitch (highness or lowness) of tones led to a discovery of a relation between pitches, and thus the tone-system in music was gradually evolved. When keys on the piano are pressed, hammers strike certain strings, setting them in motion or vibration. It is possible to observe the vibration of the larger strings, since they vibrate more slowly than the shorter and smaller (in diameter) strings. When this vibration is observed closely, the string will be seen to move back and forth. The smaller or the shorter the string, or the greater the tension, the faster it moves; the faster it moves the higher the tone. Consequently, the pitch of a tone produced by vibration of a string depends upon the number of times per second it vibrates.

It is customary to designate pitches by giving them letter names, using the series A, B, C, D, E, F, G. The pitch of middle C, according to our adopted practice of tuning, has a vibration rate of 261.6 vibrations per second; the pitch of G (2nd line, treble staff) has a vibration rate of 392 vibrations per second; and the pitch of A, one whole tone above this, has a vibration rate of 440 per second.

Clefs, then, designate the pitch of the lines and spaces of the staff. The G, or treble, clef is used to indicate the treble staff, and means that a note placed on the second line represents the pitch of a particular G, the one first above middle C. This clef is used in writing music for the violin, flute, clarinet, oboe, trumpet and other instruments having a high register.* Music for the soprano and alto voices is also written in the treble staff.

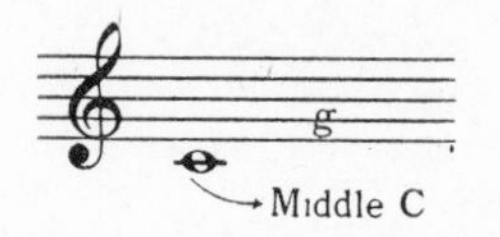

The F or bass clef is used to define the bass staff, and indicates that a note placed on the fourth line represents the pitch of the F first below middle C. This staff is used in writing music for the cello, double bass, bassoon, tuba, baritone horn, drums, and usually the trombone. Music for the bass voice, and usually that for the tenor voice, is written in the bass staff.†

* Music for all saxophones is written in the treble clef, although the larger instruments sound an octave or even two octaves lower. This is done so that a player can play all sizes without learning new fingering or a new clef.

† In chorus music, when each part appears on a separate staff, the tenor part is usually written in a treble staff though it sounds an octave lower.

The C clef, sometimes known as the tenor clef, is a movable clef; that is, the clef sign may be placed so that it may indicate any line or space as middle C. In modern notation it is always found on a line, usually the third or fourth. It is used in writing music for certain of the orchestral instruments and sometimes for the tenor voice. Music for the cello, double bass, and bassoon, although ordinarily written in the bass staff, sometimes appears in the tenor staff when passages containing high notes occur, since a continuance of the bass staff would require the addition of too many leger lines for the space provided. Some music for the trombone is also written in this clef.

The following example illustrates one use of the C clef. Note that the clef sign is placed upon the fourth line, indicating that that line is middle C.

The C clef is also used when writing for the viola, but the clef sign is placed upon the *third* line of the staff, thus making the third line represent middle C. So placed it is known as the "alto clef":

Middle C

Frequently the treble clef appears in viola music to avoid having too many leger lines.

The following example illustrates the placement of the clefs in relation to the great staff:

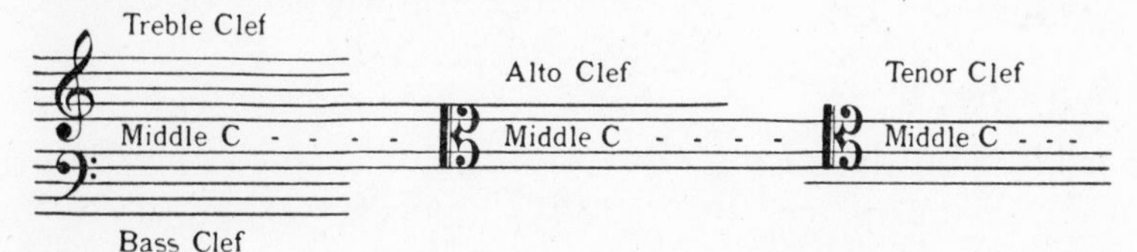

The Sharp, Flat, Double Sharp, Double Flat, and Natural

A *sharp* (♯) is a symbol which is used to raise the pitch indicated by a note one half-step. The intervals between white keys on the piano keyboard, with the exception of B-C and E-F, are whole steps and are separated by black keys which indicate the half step between. The two exceptions noted are half step intervals. Therefore no black key will be found between them. A raise in pitch indicated by a sharp is performed by sounding the black key immediately to the right, if one is present. If there is no black key the adjoining white key is used.

A *flat* (♭) is a symbol used to lower the pitch of a note one half-step. On the piano keyboard, therefore, the pitch indicated by a note may be lowered a half-step by playing the key immediately to the *left* of the key which corresponds to the letter name. Where the interval between white keys is a whole step, the black key immediately to the left sounds the flat. To the left of C and F, the adjoining white key is used.

A *double sharp* (𝄪) is a symbol used to raise the pitch of a note *two* half-steps; in other words, one whole step.

A *double flat* (♭♭) is a symbol used to lower the pitch of a note two half-steps, or one whole step.

A *natural* (♮) is a symbol used to cancel the effect of a sharp or flat which has occurred previously. A natural, therefore, has the power to either raise or lower a note, as the case may be. For example, if a natural occurs before a note that has previously been sharped, it indicates that the note is to be played "natural"—or without the sharp.

Notes and Rests

The *note* is a character expressing relative time duration. When placed on a staff it indicates that a certain tone or pitch is to be sounded for a certain relative length of time.

The value of a note (or length of time sounded) is relative in that its duration is dependent upon the *meter* (number of beats per measure) in which the composition is written, and upon the *tempo* (speed) at which the composition is played or sung.

The *rest* is a character which indicates a rhythmic silence of a certain indicated duration.

The different kinds of rests (representing periods of silence) correspond to the various kinds of notes (representing tone lengths).

Notes	Rests	Name
𝅜	𝄺	Double whole
𝅝	𝄻	Whole
𝅗𝅥	𝄼	Half
𝅘𝅥	𝄽	Quarter
𝅘𝅥𝅮	𝄾	Eighth
𝅘𝅥𝅯	𝄿	Sixteenth
𝅘𝅥𝅰	𝅀	Thirty - second
𝅘𝅥𝅱	𝅁	Sixty - fourth

Dotted Notes and Rests

If a dot is placed after a note or rest, the value of that note or rest is increased by one-half. For example, if the value of a half note is two beats, a dot placed after it (𝅗𝅥.) changes its value to three beats.

A second dot placed after a first dot adds a further value of one-half the value of the first dot. Hence if a quarter note has a value of one beat, two dots placed after it (♩..) changes its value to one and three-fourths beats.

THE MAJOR, MINOR, AND CHROMATIC SCALES

The word *scale* is derived from the Latin word *scala,* meaning ladder or stairway.

The scale which forms the basis of modern music construction is called the *diatonic* scale, and consists of a series of whole-steps and half-steps, arranged in a certain order (illustrated in the figure below). It is distinguished from the *chromatic* scale, which will be described later.

There are two methods or *modes* of arranging the tones of the diatonic scale: the *major mode* and the *minor mode.* The mode of a scale, therefore, depends upon the arrangement of whole-steps and half-steps within the limits of an octave.

The following example illustrates the arrangement of whole-steps and half-steps in a scale of the major mode, in this instance the diatonic scale of C major:

This arrangement or pattern of whole-steps and half-steps is used for all the major diatonic scales.

For a better understanding of the use of sharps and flats, and their relation to scale-building, the lines and spaces of the staff are shown below as they are related to the piano keyboard. "Middle C" is indicated by a dotted line between the treble and bass staffs. It appears on the keyboard as the C nearest the middle of the keyboard.

THE RELATION OF THE PIANO-KEYBOARD TO THE STAFF

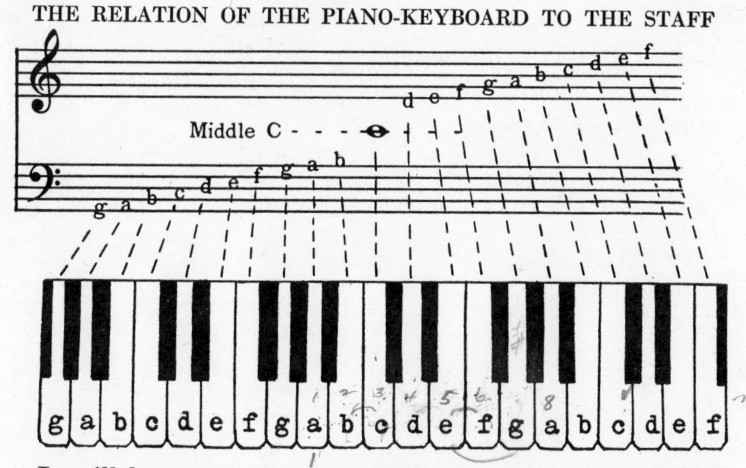

It will be noted that in building the scale of C major, only white keys on the keyboard are used. All other major scales use either sharps or flats, and these are represented on the keyboard by the black keys. With the use of these devices, it is possible to build any scale we wish, starting with any note on the staff or with any key on the piano-keyboard. Suppose for example, we wish to build a scale starting on A, second space of the treble staff. This scale then becomes known as the "scale of A," taking its name from the starting note. We now apply the major scale pattern of whole steps and half steps, using certain sharps (black keys if employing the piano) to complete the pattern of the written scale. In applying the pattern, we find that the scale of A requires the use of three sharps (or three black keys), C♯, F♯, and G♯. The following example illustrates this scale as it appears on the staff. The scale may be played on the piano by using, where the sharps are indicated, the black keys to the right of the notes sharped.

Minor Scales

There are three forms of the minor scale:

(1) The Normal (ancient) minor is used as a basis for the other two forms.

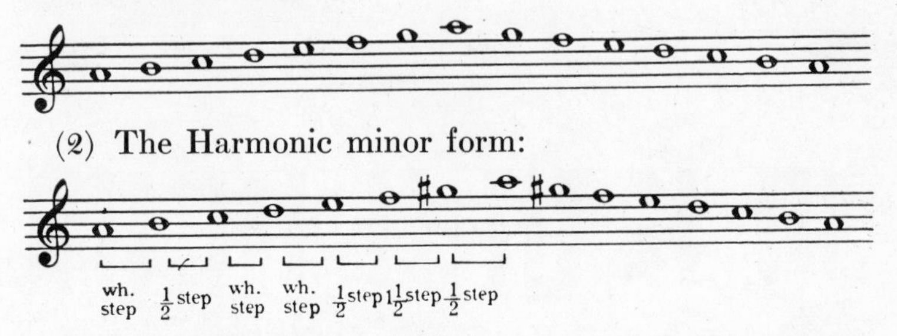

(2) The Harmonic minor form:

Note that the third and sixth tones are a half-step lower than in a major scale pattern.

(3) The Melodic minor form:

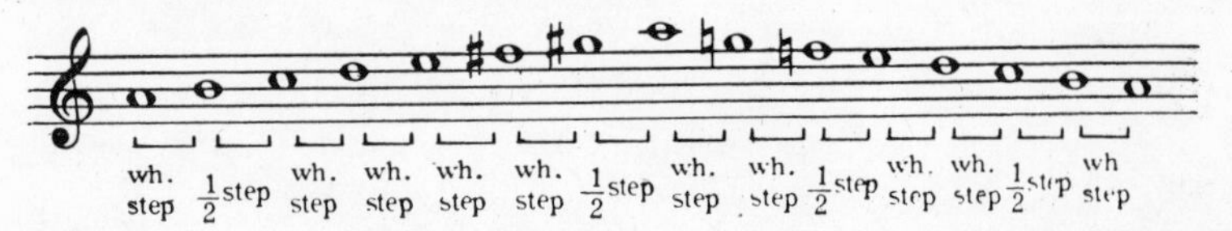

Note the difference between the ascending and the descending scales of the melodic minor form. Also note that if the third tone in the ascending scale were sharped, the scale would then be in the major mode.

A distinguishing feature by which one may determine whether a scale is major or minor is the interval or distance between the first and third tones of the scale. If the distance between them includes two whole-steps (a major third), then the scale is in the major mode. If the distance between them includes a whole-step and a half-step (a minor third), the scale is in the minor mode.

If a major scale and a minor scale having the same keynote or starting tone be compared, it will be found that they coincide at two other points; namely, at the fourth and fifth tones.

The Chromatic Scale

The *chromatic* scale is a series of adjacent half steps or semi-tones. On the piano keyboard it involves the use of all the white and black keys within the octave, numbering thirteen in all. *Chromatic signs* (accidentals) must be used to a considerable extent in the chromatic scale, as illustrated in the following example.

Since sharps raise the pitch, they are used in the ascending form of the scale. Flats serve to lower the pitch, and are therefore used in the descending form.

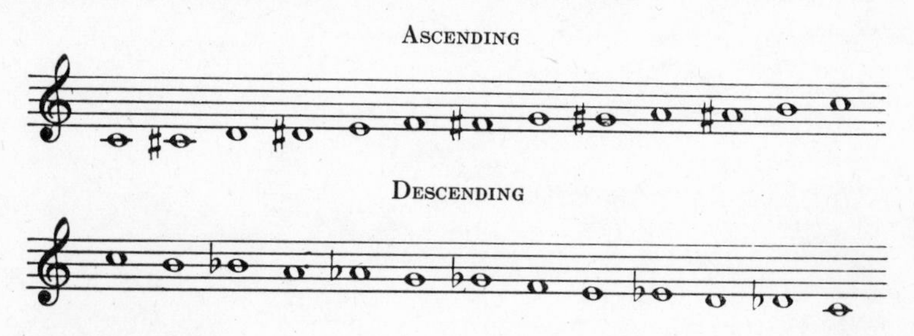

Key Signatures

All compositions, except those in the keys of C major and A minor (which use no signatures), have a key signature appearing on the staff immediately to the right of the clef sign. Signatures came into use when it was discovered that scales differing in pitch from C required the use of sharps and flats to make the necessary whole and half steps to form the scale pattern. So when compositions are written in the keys which contain these sharps or flats it is customary, in order to avoid continuous writing of accidentals, to group them on the left of each staff into what is known as the *key signature.* For example, music written in the key of G will have one sharp for its signature. Now the scale of G contains F♯, so the sharp sign in the signature is placed upon the line representing the pitch of F, which is the fifth line in the treble staff and the fourth line in the bass staff. This means that whenever the note F occurs in the composition, it must be played F♯, unless a natural sign is placed before it.

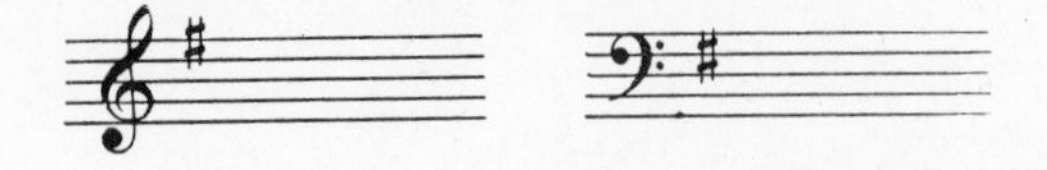

Below is a table of key signatures in the sharp keys, indicating the positions of the sharps on the staffs:

Name of Key	Number of Sharps	Names of Sharps	Position of New Sharp on Treble Staff	Position of New Sharp on Bass Staff
G	1	F	5th line	4th line
D	2	F C	3rd space	2nd space
A	3	F C G	1st space above staff	4th space
E	4	F C G D	4th line	3rd line
B	5	F C G D A	2nd space	1st space
F♯	6	F C G D A E	4th space	3rd space
C♯	7	F C G D A E B	3rd line	2nd line

If a composition is written in the key of B♭, its signature will be two flats, since the scale of B♭ contains both B♭ and E♭, in accordance with the major scale-pattern (p. 8). The flat signs are therefore placed upon the third line and fourth space in the treble staff, and upon the second line and third space in the bass staff.

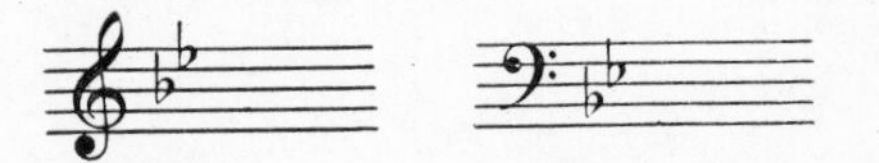

Below is a table of key signatures in the flat keys, indicating the positions of the flats on the staffs:

Name of Key	Number of Flats	Names of Flats	Position of New Flat on Treble Staff	Position of New Flat on Bass Staff
F	1	B	3rd line	2nd line
B♭	2	B E	4th space	3rd space
E♭	3	B E A	2nd space	1st space
A♭	4	B E A D	4th line	3rd line
D♭	5	B E A D G	2nd line	1st line
G♭	6	B E A D G C	3rd space	2nd space
C♭	7	B E A D G C F	1st space	1st space below staff

Signatures of Minor Mode

Signatures for the minor mode are borrowed from the major mode. It has been found most convenient to determine a minor signature by basing it on the third scale-step of the minor scale. Then assuming that this note is the tonic of a major scale, the proper signature is adopted. For example, in the scale of C minor the third scale-step is E♭, and therefore three flats will comprise the signature for C minor.

It will be noticed that this adopted signature does not exactly fit the harmonic and melodic minor scales. In the harmonic minor, an accidental is necessary at the seventh scale-step; in the melodic minor, accidentals occur in the ascending scale at the sixth and seventh scale-steps. These accidentals do not appear in the signature.

The major key represented by a minor signature is called the *relative major*. Thus E♭ major is the relative of C minor. The *relative minor* key-note of a major key may therefore be found by counting down one and one-half scale-steps from the major key-note, or conversely, by counting *up* six scale steps.*

Accidentals

As previously explained, the signature of a composition serves to indicate that certain notes in the composition are to be sharped or flatted whenever they occur. However, the indicated pitch of *any* note may be altered by inserting before it an *accidental;* that is, a sharp, flat, double sharp, double flat, or natural. The effect of this accidental holds good throughout the rest of the measure, unless it is changed by another accidental; but in subsequent measures it is assumed that its effect has lapsed and that the signature governs unless the accidental occurs again.

* When a minor mode is shown by the use of accidentals rather than by key signature, it is said to be a *tonic minor.*

RHYTHM

Meter

Music may be called a time-art, for the reason that it depends upon the lapse of time to fulfil its purpose. In order that the time-structure of music may have order and balance, it is necessary that it be carefully organized into small equal units (much the same as a clock breaks up a minute into seconds). Like poetry, music is built up by means of successions of units or measures having a definite regularity.

The Measure Signs

The measure sign, also known as the meter-signature, is located on the staff immediately to the right of the key-signature, and indicates the meter in which the music is written. It consists of two numerals, one above the other. The upper numeral indicates the number of beats in a measure; the lower numeral indicates the kind of note receiving one beat. For example, a $\frac{2}{4}$ measure sign signifies that there are two beats in a measure, and that a quarter note receives one beat.

In all music there is heard or felt a continuous pulsation, or "beat." The conductor of a chorus or of an orchestra indicates this beat with his baton. If the meter or the tempo of the music changes, the rhythmic regularity of the beat will change accordingly.

Accents

Besides the beat there occur *accents* upon one or more beats of each measure. In *simple measure* (measure having but one accent) the accent is upon the first beat only. Two kinds of measure belong to this classification, as follows:

(1) Duple or two-beat measure ($\frac{2}{4}$, $\frac{2}{8}$, $\frac{2}{2}$): a strong beat followed by a weak beat (1_2).

(2) Triple or three-beat measure ($\frac{3}{4}$, $\frac{3}{8}$, $\frac{3}{2}$): a strong beat followed by two weak beats (123).

Compound measure is a combination of two or more simple measures, and contains two or more accents, the first of which is always the strongest. There are four kinds of compound measure:

(1) Quadruple or four-beat measure ($\frac{4}{4}$). The first and third beats are accented (1234).

(2) Sextuple or six-beat measure ($\frac{6}{8}$). The first and fourth beats are accented (123456).

(3) Compound triple or nine-beat measure ($\frac{9}{8}$). The first, fourth, and seventh beats are accented (123456789).

(4) Compound quadruple or twelve-beat measure ($\frac{12}{8}$). The first, fourth, seventh, and tenth beats are accented (123456789 10 11 12).

The Bar and Double Bar

The purpose of the bar is to separate the notes of a composition into an orderly arrangement, according to the meter in which the music is written. The space between two bars is called a *measure*.

The purpose of the double bar is to separate the various strains, or musical thoughts, of a composition. The space between double bars in music may be likened to the paragraph in literature.

The Triplet and Duplet

A triplet is a group of three notes of the same kind executed in the same amount of time as a group of two notes of the same kind at their usual value. A figure 3 accompanies a triplet, indicating that the three notes are to be played as a triplet. A duplet, accompanied by a figure 2, is a group of two notes given the time value of three notes of the same kind.

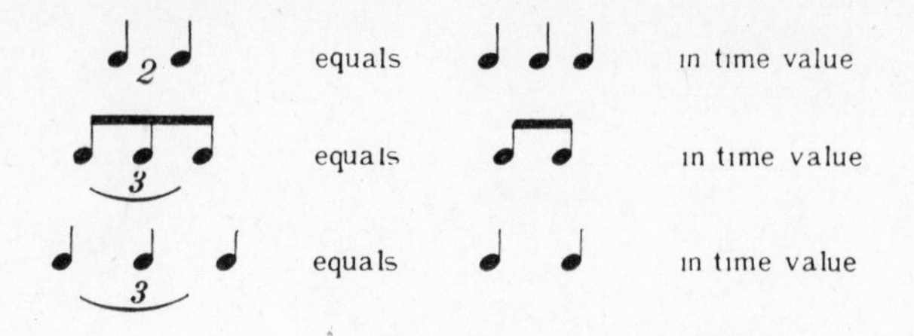

The use of a triplet or duplet involves a subdivision of the rhythm different from that designated for the piece of music as a whole. The main rhythm goes on unbroken, but the manner of subdivision is altered for the purpose of contrast.

[For selected references for Chapter I see page 139]

CHAPTER II

HARMONY

"Of the nine, the loveliest three,
Are painting, music, poetry,
But thou art freest of the free,
Matchless muse of harmony."
GRILLPARZER

HARMONY in music means exactly the same thing as harmony used in any other sense, the fitting together of various parts into an agreeable unit. When two people marry and get along well together, we speak of it as an harmonious union; and when the people in an office work well together, we say they work in harmony. And so it is with music. When we put two tones together and they sound well, we call it harmony; when two other tones sound discordant, we speak of it as unharmonious. Harmony in life results from the compliant natures of individuals; harmony in music is caused no less by natural laws. The vibrations of a string, as was pointed out in chapter one, may be measured and counted. Another string, to sound in harmony with it, must vibrate in a certain proportional speed to the first. The laws governing the harmonic agreement resulting from the ratio between two or more rates of vibration are the laws of harmony.

For all of us music would be quite uninteresting without harmony. This is because we are so accustomed to hearing it. If we had lived in the days of Caesar, we would have been quite content to sing or play the melody only. Today however, arrangers are emphasizing the harmony to such an extent that it is probably more important to us than any other element of music. To illustrate, one of our well known church organists played "Home Sweet Home" as a prelude, using modern harmony instead of the original, and the audience failed to recognize the tune!

Harmony might be compared to the costumes of an actress. In one play she dons the garb of Queen Elizabeth because it conforms to the part she is playing; another play might require her to wear tennis shorts. She is, however, still the same actress. We may take a familiar tune and harmonize it in several different ways. We know it is the same tune but in its strange dress find it scarcely recognizable, since we learned to know it not only by the melody, but by the harmony and rhythm as well. The development of harmony has followed the actress in another direction also. In the colonial days, she wore a hoop skirt. As time went on, the hoop skirt went out of style, and she wore a shorter, narrower skirt. Harmony likewise has developed new styles. We are no longer content with the old familiar sounds. We want newer, stranger, and more startling combinations.

Compared to the thousands of years man has sung or played the melody only, the practice of harmony is still young. Yet in the first three hundred years of its existence, it had so accustomed itself to the ears of its hearers, that it had assumed fairly fixed forms which we recognize as classical harmony. Perhaps in a hundred years or so these familiar sounds will seem hopelessly quaint and simple, and the "ultra-modern" music of today will have become the "classical" music of our great grandchildren.

In order to appreciate harmony, it is not entirely necessary for one to know its rules. Some knowledge of its structure is a valuable aid to discrimination however, and therefore a brief background will be presented including some of the standard rules, methods of producing simple harmonies, and the terminology of the subject.

NAMES OF THE SCALE-TONES

Each step of the diatonic scale has a specific name. These names are a part of the language of music, and should be memorized. Arranged according to their relative importance in harmony, they are:

1st tone—Tonic (key-note).
5th tone (Perf. 5th above Tonic)—Dominant.
4th tone (Perf. 5th below Tonic)—Subdominant.
2nd tone (Perf. 5th above Dom.)—Supertonic.
6th tone (midway between Ton. and Subdom.)—Submediant.
3rd tone (midway between Ton. and Dom.)—Mediant.
7th tone—Leading-tone.

The Tonic, Dominant, and Subdominant, being of greater harmonic importance than the other scale-steps, are called *principal* scale-steps.

The Supertonic, Submediant, and Mediant are called *subordinate* scale-steps.

The Leading-tone has no special classification.

INTERVALS

The difference in pitch between two tones is measured by the number of steps between the notes representing the tones on the staff, and is called an *interval.*

Intervals are always counted upward along the diatonic major scale of the lower tone. The number of the scale-step represented by the upper tone determines the numerical name of the interval.

Diatonic Intervals

Diatonic or natural intervals are those in which the upper tone represents a major scale-step of the lower tone, the lower being considered as tonic. These intervals have the following numerical names: unison (or prime), second, third, fourth, fifth, sixth, seventh, octave, ninth, tenth, etc. They are divided into two classes—*perfect* and *major*.

The perfect intervals are: unison, fourth, fifth, and octave. The major intervals are: second, third, sixth and seventh.

Chromatic Intervals

Chromatic intervals are those in which the upper tone does not agree with the notes of the major scale based on the lower tone.

When a perfect interval is extended by placing an accidental before the upper tone, the interval becomes *augmented.* When a perfect interval is contracted in similar manner, it becomes *diminished.*

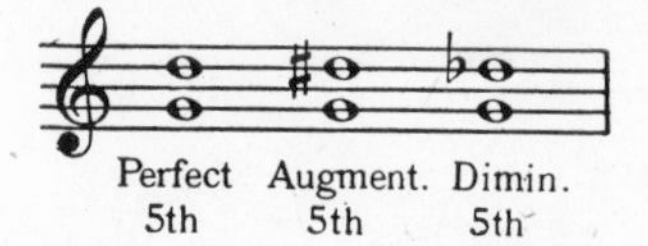

When any *major* interval is extended by an accidental, it is called *augmented,* the same as an extended perfect interval; but when contracted by an accidental, a major interval becomes *minor.* If a minor interval is contracted by one half-step, or if a major interval is contracted by two half-steps, the result will be a *diminished* interval. Thus:

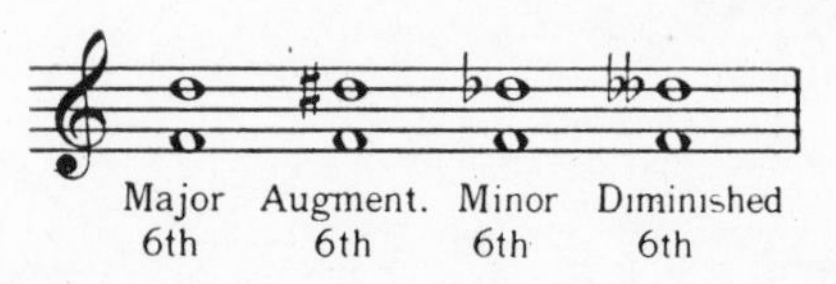

It should be remembered when dealing with chromatic intervals, that the letter names of the notes must remain unchanged. In the above example, the upper note of the augmented sixth must be D♯ rather than E♭, because an E♭ would identify the interval as a minor 7th. Similarly, the diminished sixth must have D♭♭ for its upper note—not C.

Below is a list of intervals, and some of their forms:

Unison: Perfect, Augmented, Diminished.
Second: Major, Augmented, Minor, Diminished.
Third: Major, Augmented, Minor, Diminished.
Fourth: Perfect, Augmented, Diminished.
Fifth: Perfect, Augmented, Diminished.
Sixth: Major, Augmented, Minor, Diminished.
Seventh: Major, Augmented, Minor, Diminished.
Octave: Perfect, Augmented, Diminished.

Inversion of Intervals

To *invert* means to turn upside down or to reverse the order. In the inversion of intervals, the position of the tones is reversed so that the lower tone becomes the upper. It is done by changing one of the tones of the interval to its octave position nearest the other tone.

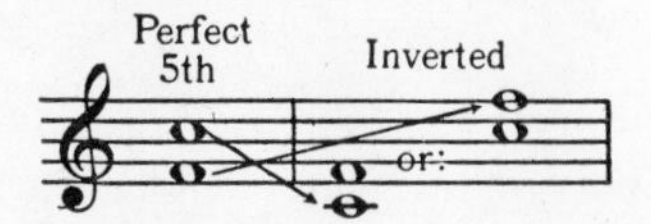

It will be noted that the above example, a perfect fifth, remains a perfect interval in its inverted form. The same is true of all perfect intervals; their inversions are perfect also. In the case of other intervals however, not only is the size of the interval changed, but the *quality* as well. Major intervals become minor; augmented become diminished. The principle is elaborated below:

Interval	Inverted
Perfect unison	Perfect octave
Major second	Minor seventh
Minor second	Major seventh
Major third	Minor sixth
Minor third	Major sixth
Perfect fourth	Perfect fifth
Perfect fifth	Perfect fourth
Major sixth	Minor third
Minor sixth	Major third
Major seventh	Minor second
Minor seventh	Major second
Perfect octave	Perfect unison

Consonance and Dissonance

A consonance is an interval which sounds well to the ear, and is complete in itself. That is, it does not leave the hearer with the impression that something is to follow.

A dissonance is an interval which sounds unfinished. It gives a feeling that another combination of tones must follow in order to satisfy the ear.

The inversions of consonant intervals are also consonant, and the inversions of dissonant intervals are dissonant. Below is a list of the consonances and dissonances. Since major and minor thirds and sixths are not perfect intervals, they are classified as *imperfect* consonances.

CONSONANCES

Perfect octaves and their inversions, perfect unisons.
Perfect fifths and their inversions, perfect fourths.
Major thirds and their inversions, minor sixths. } Imperfect
Minor thirds and their inversions, major sixths. }

DISSONANCES

Major seconds and their inversions, minor sevenths.
Minor seconds and their inversions, major sevenths.
All augmented and diminished intervals.

Chords and Triads

A chord is defined as a combination of three or more tones having certain recognized pitch relations with each other. Simple chords are made up of the tones of a diatonic major or minor scale. If other tones than these are used, the chords are known as *altered* or *chromatic* chords.

The skeleton of a chord is the perfect fifth. The most satisfactory to the ear and hence the most logical tone to complete the chord is the third. This three-tone structure (any tone as a basis, with its fifth and third) is called a *triad*.

The lowest tone of a triad is called the *root*, which may be any step of the diatonic scale.

A chord receives its name from the scale step occupied by its root. Triads are divided into two classes, as follows:

1. Primary Triads
   - Tonic: do-mi-sol
   - Dominant: sol-ti-re
   - Subdominant: fa-la-do
2. Secondary Triads
   - Supertonic: re-fa-la
   - Mediant: mi-sol-ti
   - Submediant: la-do-mi

Triads are also designated by Roman numerals, representing the number of the scale-step occupied by their roots. The large numerals indicate major triads; the small numerals, minor triads. The difference between major and minor triads rests in the size of the interval between the root and the third. If there are two whole steps between these tones, the triad is major; if there are one and one-half steps, the triad is minor. Both primary and secondary triads contain perfect fifths. The triad erected on the seventh tone consists of two minor thirds, and so does not contain a perfect fifth. This triad is neither primary nor secondary. It is denoted by a small Roman numeral, with a degree sign showing that it is a diminished triad.

The form of a triad may be altered by placing any note of the triad an octave above or below its normal position in the triad. Notice that this usually inverts one or more intervals in the triad. The following example shows several possible forms of the F major triad:

Inversion of Triads

The continued use of chords in their fundamental position tends to become dull and uninteresting. The inversion of chords contributes to variety and contrast in music, and also makes possible smooth and graceful chord-progressions.

There are two inversions possible in every triad. The first inversion is made by transferring the root to its octave position above the third and fifth:

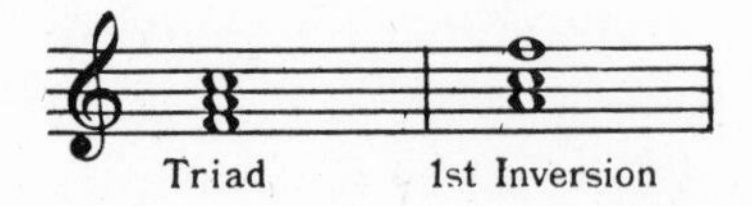

The second inversion of a triad is made by transferring the root and third to their octave positions above the fifth:

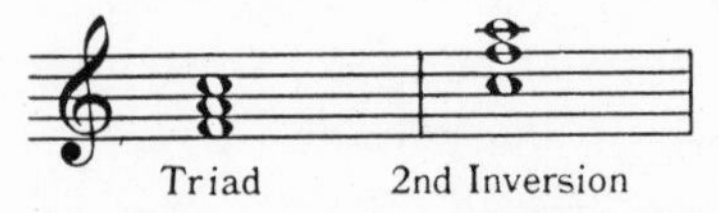

Four parts, or voices, are generally used in writing music: namely, soprano, alto, tenor, and bass. Since the triad (3-tone chord) contains the fundamental notes of a chord, it may be enlarged to a 4-tone chord by duplicating, or doubling, one of its tones. Certain rules are to be observed in the writing of 4-part harmony, chief of which are as follows:

1. The treble clef is used for the soprano and alto parts; the bass clef, for the tenor and bass parts. Soprano and bass are called *outer* parts; alto and tenor are called *inner* parts.

2. The root is the best tone to double in a primary triad.

3. The third is best to double in a secondary triad, although it is permissible to double the root.

4. The fifth of a chord should seldom be doubled.

5. Inverted forms may be used (see illustration); in fact it is desirable to use them for the sake of variety.

6. The *fifth* of a primary triad is sometimes omitted, and the root of the chord tripled. The *third* must be included in every chord, however.

7. Parts must rarely cross; that is, a soprano note should not be written below an alto note, an alto note should not be written below a tenor note, etc.

8. An alto note in a chord should not be located more than an octave from either the soprano or tenor notes. It is permissible, however, to write the bass and tenor more than an octave apart.

9. Successive fifths and successive octaves are not to be used except when a chord is repeated exactly.

10. It is best to avoid wide leaps in any part except the bass. This part usually takes the root of each chord and is therefore permitted to make wide leaps.

11. The leading-tone should ascend rather than descend. It usually ascends to the tonic.

12. The soprano and bass parts should move in contrary direction whenever possible.

The following examples illustrate how four-tone chords may be erected from a triad as a basis:

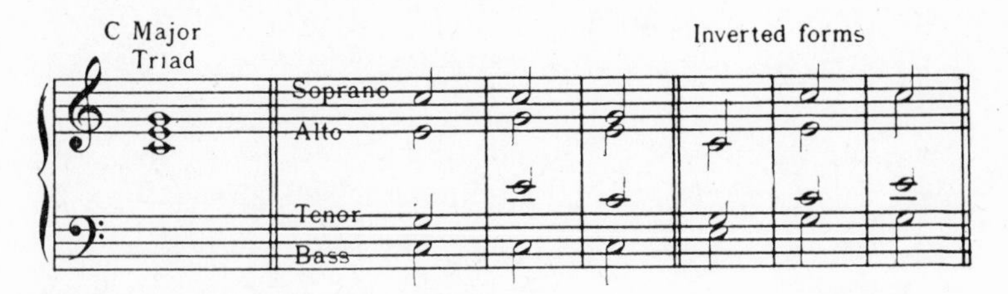

The Dominant-Seventh Chord

By adding the interval of a minor third to the top of a dominant triad, the chord becomes a dominant-seventh chord. It is so called because the distance between the root and the upper note is the interval of a seventh. Since the Roman numeral V represents the dominant step of a scale, the dominant-seventh chord is designated by $\overset{7}{\text{V}}$—called "five-seven."

Three inversions of the dominant-seventh chord are possible, as follows:

First inversion ($\overset{7}{\text{V}}_1$—called "five-seven-one"): —Bass takes the *third* of the chord.

Second inversion ($\overset{7}{\text{V}}_2$—called "five-seven-two"): —Bass takes the *fifth* of the chord.

Third inversion ($\overset{7}{\text{V}}_3$—called "five-seven-three"): —Bass takes the *seventh* of the chord.

The following example illustrates the dominant-seventh chord and its inversions:

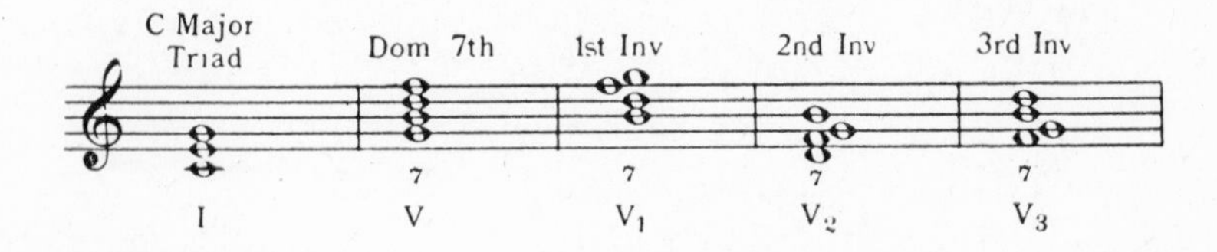

The Cadence

Musical sentences in a simple song usually consist of eight-measure phrases, divided into two parts of four measures each. At the middle of the eight-measure sentence a slight pause or interruption of rhythm occurs, usually upon a dominant chord (the V). The progression upon which this pause occurs is called the *semicadence,* or *half-cadence.*

The second part of the sentence closes with the progression V-I, giving a feeling that the musical thought is completed. This closing progression is called the *authentic,* or *perfect cadence.*

OLD FOLKS AT HOME

Chord-Progression

Let us now turn our attention to the subject of *chord-progressions;* e.g., the art of placing chords in a familiar, well-ordered succession.

Many modern composers do not limit themselves to fixed rules of chord-progression. The established rules of harmony cannot be applied to all the descriptive or impressionistic music being written today. Nevertheless, modern composers have studied those rules during early periods of their careers, so that they are familiar with them, even though they may disregard them. It is fundamental to a knowledge of harmony that music students familiarize themselves with certain rules, and know how to apply them.

All harmonized music involves the progression of chords. If two chords have at least one tone in common, they are said to be related, and generally a chord progression to a related chord creates an effect that is satisfying to the ear. Below are listed the more important rules governing chord-progression:

Rules for Chord Progressions

1. A tonic chord (the I) may progress into any other chord of the same key or of another key.
2. A dominant chord (the V) usually progresses only into a tonic chord; e. g., V–I.
3. A subdominant chord (the IV) usually progresses either to the I or the V; e. g., IV–I or IV–V.
4. A submediant chord (the VI) may progress to any chord of its own key, excepting the I.
5. A supertonic chord (the II) progresses most smoothly to the V or the VI; e. g., II–V or II–VI. The best progressions *into* the II are: IV–II, VI–II, and I–II.
6. A mediant chord (the III) is ordinarily used only when the leading tone as soprano progresses to the 6th scale-step. The III then progresses to the IV. When the III places the 5th scale-step as soprano, the III may progress to the VI or the IV.

Below is a summary of the best chord progressions for each fundamental chord or triad. These rules do not apply to inversions.

The I progresses to any other chord, but most frequently to the V, IV, VI, and III.

The II progresses to the V or VI.

The III progresses to the VI or IV.

The IV progresses to the V or I.

The V progresses to the I.

The VI progresses to the IV, III, II, or V.

[For selected references for Chapter II see page 139]

CHAPTER III

THE HISTORY OF MUSIC

"Time wrecks the proudest piles we raise,
The towers, the domes, the temples fall,
The fortress crumbles and decays,
One breath of song outlives them all."

OLIVER WENDELL HOLMES

MUSIC, unlike other great arts and sciences, was not *invented,* it was *discovered.* Existing already in nature, it required only some one who could interpret and draw out the essentials of melody, rhythm, and harmony which make up our scheme of music. Music exists in the sighing of the wind, the swaying of the trees, the dashing of the waves upon the shore, and booming in the caves and caverns of the coast. Rhythm is inherent in everything we do and see; melody dwells in the lilt of the birds; and harmony too, reveals itself to those who have become sensitive to its presence.

The discovery of music occurred so long ago that man has no true record of its beginning. We are able to surmise that music existed as long ago as 3500 B.C. For many years of course it existed in a very primitive form, and it was not until comparatively recent times that we have had music in its present form. For example, we have had our five-line staff for only about four hundred years, and the piano for only a little over two-hundred-fifty. However, from the very first, music has been closely associated with the intimate lives of all peoples. It has served as a comfort in times of sorrow, and has always been the ultimate expression of joy. Probably no medium of expression is chosen so extensively and universally by mankind as an emotional release, nor has any other art made a more significant contribution to life.

Man's first musical discoveries may have been vocal or instrumental, but it is probable that both came into being about the same time. Perhaps some form of drum was fashioned from a hollow log with an animal skin stretched over the top. Perhaps musical sounds were suggested by the calling of birds, the whistling of the wind, or the rumbling sound produced by pounding a hollow tree. The twang of a bow string may have suggested the idea for the primitive harp, and some curious soul may have discovered that he could make a loud and more or less musical sound by blowing in the horn of an animal.

These first attempts at music making must have been quite crude and inartistic. Man had not yet learned to organize sounds in any definite pattern. He probably took part in a crude dance, however, and as the rhythm of dancing became more definite and regular, a more careful arrangement of sounds followed. The discovery was made that pleasing rhythmic effects could be produced by grouping successions of beats upon the drum in various ways, and in this way meter must have originated. Chanting voices must have risen and fallen in pitch, according to the degree of emotional feeling, giving rise to the idea of vocal melody.

An example of this primitive understanding of the nature of music may be seen in the musical attempts of the American Indian. Music was an important part of his tribal and individual life. He had a song for almost everything about him, a song for the lakes, the trees, for fire, for his weapons, for the wild animals he hunted, and for the thousand and one objects he met in his daily life. As time went on the number of songs steadily increased, and of course, no one could tell from whence they came or how they were developed. Indian boys were carefully taught the songs of the tribes and clans, and these songs were passed on from one family to the next, and from generation to generation. In this way the young Indians learned the history of their people.

Indian themes will serve as an example also to show the influence primitive tunes have exerted on our modern music. Many composers of recent years have used melodies of Indian origin as the basis for larger compositions. Dvorak, for example, found inspiration in these primitive melodies for his "String Quartet in F Major." Other composers have used old Indian melodies from which they have constructed beautiful songs. Lieurance in his "By the Waters of Minnetonka" and Cadman with his "Land of the Sky Blue Water" have done this very cleverly and artistically.

So, in order to get a picture of the development of music through the ages, we will begin with the most ancient musical system known, and trace briefly its history.

THE ANCIENT PERIOD

China

The Chinese were probably the first people to devise a complete music system. These people, however, scarcely ever used music as a means of expressing emotion and beauty, but looked upon it mainly as a science, which offered a field for experimentation. Their music was quite complicated, as may well be imagined when we learn that their system made use of eighty-four scales. The great Chinese teacher, Confucius, exerted much influence upon the music of his people. He composed songs and was a performer upon the lute.

Many of the Chinese wind instruments are made from bamboo, for there are large forests of this wood growing in China. The most popular of the stringed instruments is the *kin,* a primitive guitar. Small bells are attached to the instrument, which are used to make a clanging noise as an accompaniment to the plucking of the strings. The trumpet is also used by the Chinese, especially in battle or in religious ceremonies.

The Chinese prefer gongs, cymbals, bells, and drums to all other instruments. They have little or no feeling for melody and harmony, but love to make loud clanging noises. They think this drives away dragons and evil spirits.

So great is the respect and reverence of the Chinese for their ancestors that they have refused to add many new things to their ancient music system, preferring to be content with their first ideas and inventions. But today China is beginning to accept new ideas and is showing a desire to progress with the rest of the world in various fields of culture.

Egypt

The Egyptians were very fond of music, and we learn from pictures and inscriptions found in ancient Egyptian tombs that they had large choruses of singers and played upon a variety of musical instruments, the most popular of which was the harp. The trumpet, flute, and drum also were known, but were somewhat different from those in use today.

Music was cultivated in Egypt as early as 3000 B.C., and reached its highest development during the Golden Age, 1500-1200 B.C. After that time, Egyptian music deteriorated steadily, finally losing its national character when Persia conquered Egypt in 525 B.C.

Assyria

Assyrian music was an outgrowth of the culture of Babylon, an ancient city on the Euphrates river, dating from 3000 B. C. Babylon became a part of the Assyrian Empire about 1300 B.C. The musical instruments used by the Assyrians were similar to the ancient Egyptian, but were made so that they could be strapped to the body and carried in processions. The most widely used was the *dulcimer*, an instrument played by striking strings with small hammers. The *double-pipes* were used in both Assyria and Egypt. This instrument resembles two flutes, connected at one end by a single mouthpiece.

The Assyrians had such a high regard for music that when musicians were taken prisoners in war their lives were spared.

India

Early development of a music-system in India is apparent from references and descriptions in sacred Hindu books, dating from about 2000 B.C. The music of these people was more advanced and complicated than that of the ancient Chinese. The Hindoos produced many religious songs which, combined with dancing, occupied a place of importance in their ceremonies. A variety of musical instruments were in use in India. The national instrument was the *vina,* a long hollow tube with five or six strings stretched over several adjustable bridges, and played by plucking the strings. The resonance of the instrument was increased by attaching a hollow gourd at each end.

Palestine

Hebrew music was probably derived from that of Egypt and Assyria, but did not reach the artistic development of the latter. Music was considered inspirational and was much used in Hebrew worship. Large choirs of voices accompanied by instruments performed in the temples. The fullest musical development was reached during the reign of King Solomon, when a group of four thousand musicians assisted in religious ceremonies. The instruments used by the Hebrews were much the same as those of the Egyptians and Assyrians, but apparently drums were not used at all. The principal instrument used in religious services was the *shofar,* a trumpet made from a ram's horn.

Greek Music

The word music meant to the ancient Greeks the entire field of the arts and sciences. It stood not only for singing and the playing of instruments, but included poetry, dancing, the drama, astronomy, and mathematics. The word takes its name from the Muses. Greek mythology tells us that the nine Muses were the daughters of Zeus, the supreme god of the Greeks, and that each of these Muses represented some particular art or science. For example, Terpsichore was the Muse of the Dance; Urania was the Muse of Astronomy; Clio was the Muse of History and Epic Poetry; etc.

The music-system of the ancient Greeks was more highly developed than that of any other ancient people. They were the first to attempt musical notation, but did not use a staff as we do. They simply described the tones by using names for them. Unfortunately, extremely few examples have survived through the ages, and their system of writing music was not accurate enough to provide us with much knowledge about its practical side. Hence, our knowledge of Greek music comes to us through the works which have been written *about* their music, rather than from actual examples.

The basis of the Greek scales was the tetrachord (*tetra*=four, *chord*=string), corresponding to the four strings of the *lyre,* the favorite stringed instrument of the Greeks. The tetrachord is a group of four tones within the interval of a fourth, consisting of two whole-steps and one half-step (do-fa). Three kinds of tetrachords were commonly used by the Greeks: Dorian, Phrygian, and Lydian. These tetrachords formed the primary modes, those most commonly used. There were seven or more modes employed, however, whereas in our own music-system we have but two, major and minor. Tones which correspond approximately* to the three Greek tetrachords are as follows:

Dorian, E F-G-A; Phrygian, A-B C-D; Lydian, C-D-E F.†

By combining two tetrachords the Greek scales were formed. Thus, if we put together two Lydian tetrachords we have a scale which corresponds roughly to one of our own major scales:

C-D-E F — G-A-B C

If we combine a Phrygian and a Dorian tetrachord the result will be the Normal or ancient minor scale, which is used as a basis for the minor scales in use today:

A-B C-D — E F-G-A

The Greeks thought of their scales as progressing downward rather than upward, as we reckon our scales.

Each of the many Greek modes had its particular use. One was used for religious music, one for military music, one for funeral music, one for festivals and joyous occasions, and so on.

Music became the subject for much study and theorizing among the ancient Greek philosophers. Perhaps the most important writer on music was Pythagoras, who lived in the sixth century B. C. He is given credit for the invention of the *monochord,* a musical instrument with one string and provided with a movable bridge.

The national instrument of the Greeks was the *lyre,* a small harp originally made by stretching strings across a tortoise shell. At first, four strings were used; later, more were added to these.

Choral music was sung in unison. Part-singing was unknown to the Greeks, so far as we know.

The Greeks loved beauty. They expressed it in every-

* Because the intervals between, and hence pitch, of tones were slightly different from our modern scale.

† The hyphen indicates a whole step.

thing they made or did. Their unsurpassed masterpieces of sculpture and architecture testify to the high artistic ideals and accomplishments of these ancient peoples. While their musical art did not reach the perfect fulfillment of their sculpture, yet it occupied a place of great importance in their lives. To them it was another way of revealing beauty.

Roman Music

The Romans did not have the artistic ideals or the creative ability in affairs of art which the Greeks possessed. The people of Rome were interested mostly in war, in road building, and in law-making. But when Greece was conquered by the Romans the classic influence of the Greeks crept into Rome; Greek teachers were employed to teach music, architecture, and sculpture. Rome had conquered many nations and had become immensely wealthy. It was natural to employ this wealth in beautifying with sculpture and pleasing architecture the first city of the world. It was natural too for the rich to indulge in the musical art, at least to the extent of having skilled musicians play for them at their banquets and entertainments. Among the spoils of conquered nations were many kinds of musical instruments. The Romans liked especially to bring back instruments which could be used in military processions, such as trumpets and drums. From these and other instruments they borrowed ideas and made their own according to similar patterns.

The Romans showed little talent for composing music, but many of them became quite skillful as players. Schools were established for the training of musicians, and contests were held in which prizes were offered to those who could play the fastest or blow the loudest.

Eventually music in Rome declined to a less serious level. Instead of the stately choral music which had been used as an accompaniment for the classical Greek tragedies, lively festive music was sung by large groups of singers for the delight of the guests at fashionable banquets. In the theaters, pantomime with orchestral and vocal accompaniment became popular. The Romans were too fond of the excitement of the ampitheater to enjoy Greek plays. They liked music best when it was noisy and lively.

EARLY CHURCH MUSIC

During the first few centuries after the birth of Christ, the combined culture of the Greeks and Romans continued to rank first among the civilizations of Europe. Then came the years known as the Dark Ages (approximately from 500 to 1300 A.D.) During this period there was little or no progress in the arts and sciences. Barbarous or half-civilized tribes from all Europe flocked into the various provinces of the Roman Empire, settling there and introducing their unpolished customs and modes of living. Culture became engaged in a struggle for its very existence, and was only kept alive by the Christian monks of the monasteries. These scholarly men devoted much time to the pursuit of learning and writing.

About 384 A.D., St. Ambrose, a Bishop of the Christian Church, wrote what became known as the Ambrosian Chant. It is said to be the first piece of Christian music ever composed. St. Ambrose collected suitable melodies which he had heard and combined them with words which told about the life of Christ. The music had none of the form which exists in our music today. Music notation used at that time consisted of a series of marks resembling shorthand characters, which were written above the words to indicate the rise and fall of the voice. It is thought that St. Ambrose used in his Church music four diatonic scales, taken from the Greek scales.

For a long time the use of musical instruments was discouraged because they were associated with the worldly paganism that had so long dominated Roman life. But the value of choral music in the ritual worship of the Church came to be recognized, and many monks with musical talent turned their attention to the writing of original hymns and chants.

A type of pipe-organ, the *hydraulis*, was invented in the 2nd century B.C. by Ktesibios of Alexandria. The instrument is so named because the supply of air was secured by means of water pressure. A clay model of a hydraulis, which gives a fairly good idea of its construction, was discovered at Carthage in 1885. This primitive pipe-organ came to be used in church worship about the 7th century, A.D.

For about 200 years after the death of St. Ambrose, the monks used the Ambrosian Chant as a pattern for their compositions. The next important advance in music was made by Pope Gregory, who headed the Christian Church from 590 to 604 A.D. He added to the four scales used by St. Ambrose, four more, all of which were given Greek names. The music which he originated was a step forward in musical progress, and is known as the Gregorian Chant, sometimes called *plain-song*. His system inspired new interest in ritual music. Monks came long distances to learn more about the new method. From his newly-invented music-system, Gregory built up an elaborate ritual containing mysterious and impressive chants.

Beginning of Part-Writing

During all this time there had been no part-singing in Church music. It was all sung in unison. One of the first, or perhaps the first, to introduce part-singing was Hucbald (840-930), a Benedictine monk from Flanders. He has been called the father of systematic harmony, and his works show that he made use of staff lines to indicate pitch. Parallel fourths and fifths constituted his characteristic harmonies. This crude system of part-writing was called *organum,* a word which probably is derived from *organon,* from which comes our modern term *organ.* Successive fourths and fifths sound disagreeable to us, but were considered good taste for several centuries during the Middle Ages. For many years thirds and sixths were held discordant and were not used.

Guido d'Arezzo

During the 11th century, another important step was taken in the progress of music. Guido d'Arezzo, also a Benedictine monk, originated *solmization,* which means a series of syllables used as names for tones of the scale. These syllables were *ut, re, mi, fa, sol, la.* The syllable *do* was substituted for *ut* about 1670. Guido took these syllables from the lines of a hymn. Each line of this hymn began with a tone one degree higher than the previous one. Guido selected the first syllable in each of the six lines to represent the tones of his scale, as follows:

*Ut*queant laxis,
*Re*sonare fibris,
*Mi*ra gestorum,
*Fa*muli tuorum,
*Sol*ve polluti,
*La*bia reatum.

This hymn was written to St. John the Baptist, whose name in Latin is Sancte Ioannes. It is probable that the syllable *ti,* the seventh degree of our modern scale, was derived from *si,* the initials of this Latin name.

Thus, Guido d'Arezzo had invented a six-tone scale, or *hexachord,* an extension of the Greek tetrachord (four-tone scale). Guido collected all the knowledge about music that he could find and wrote a book about it. He became a great teacher, and succeeded in teaching his pupils sight reading. As an aid in the use of syllables, Guido invented a system in which the finger tips and joints of the fingers represented different syllables and tones, and every fourth tone was the beginning of a new scale. In music history this system is referred to as the *Guidonian Hand*.

Credit is given Guido d'Arezzo for the invention of a four-line staff, in which both lines and spaces were used for indicating tones. The second line was red, and represented the tone F. The fourth line was yellow, and represented C. The first and third lines were black. Eventually, Guido discarded the use of colored lines, and placed the letters C and F at the beginning of the lines instead. Writers of music continued to experiment with staffs having various numbers of lines, some having as many as eleven and some fifteen. The five-line staff has been in use since about 1500 A.D.

Franco of Cologne

As singers became more expert in their art, they tended to ornament their melodies by singing two or more parts together. This caused a great deal of confusion, since there had not yet been established a system of measured music. About 1200, a monk named Franco of Cologne wrote a set of laws providing for measure, notation, and part-writing. Some of his fundamental laws of harmony are in use today. His system recognized the third as a consonance, while the major and minor seventh, the second, and the augmented fourth were classified as the only dissonances.

The meter-signatures used by Franco were as follows:

Triple meter (tempus perfectum), ○
Duple meter (tempus imperfectum), C

SECULAR MUSIC OF THE MIDDLE AGES

Troubadours, Trouveres, and Jongleurs

Let us now leave the subject of Church music for the moment and dwell a little upon another type of music — the secular or popular music of the Middle Ages.

During the 12th and 13th centuries, there emerged from southern France a group of minstrels or song-poets known as the *troubadours*. Of the wealthy noble class, they applied themselves to the composing of poetry and music for the enjoyment of their leisure, rather than as a means of earning a livelihood. The troubadours were organized as a brotherhood or fraternity, their membership including several kings and princes. Their songs were of a romantic, sentimental nature; they enjoyed singing and playing love songs.

The troubadours did not always sing and play their own songs, but very often employed the services of professional musicians known as *jongleurs,* who were of a lower social order. In medieval times wealthy lords and barons lived in castles. When a troubadour paid a visit to a friend's establishment he would take with him a company of jongleurs, who would sing and play his compositions for the entertainment of his host. On such an occasion, a troubadour considered it beneath his dignity and position in society to perform the song himself. Then, too, the jongleurs were clever, and no doubt they could in most cases give a better performance than the troubadour himself. The jongleurs were often accomplished in other kinds of entertainment, such as acrobatics, dancing, juggling, and sleight-of-hand tricks. (The word jongleur means juggler in English.) These roving minstrels would journey from town to town earning their livelihood with their songs and amusing antics. Eventually, the songs of the jongleurs became so poor in quality that these entertainers, once welcomed everywhere, were no longer admitted to the monasteries, and were not even allowed to sing and play in the streets during Lent. They became more or less a class of beggars and rogues, finally losing their identity as minstrels.

Another class of musicians similar to the troubadours

flourished in the northern part of France. They were called *trouveres,* and their membership was drawn not only from the noble or wealthy class, but also from other classes as well. Their songs were concerned usually with the deeds of great heroes, but they wrote many religious lyrics as well as heroic ballads and epics. The trouveres were active in an area where there were many monasteries, in which the monks were composing and teaching music. So it was natural that their style should be influenced to some extent by the church music of that period. It is probable also that some of the original works of the trouveres may have exercised some effect on church music. Like the troubadours, the trouveres quite frequently employed jongleurs to perform their songs for them.

The name of one trouvere stands out as the most famous—Adam de la Halle (1240-87), who composed "Robin et Marion," considered to be the first comic opera.

The Minnesingers and Meistersingers

In southern Germany, during the 12th and 13th centuries, there flourished a class of poet-musicians corresponding almost exactly to the troubadours of southern France. They were called the *minnesingers,* the word being derived from *minne* (love), for at first nearly all of their songs were love songs. Later they composed and sang religious songs, heroic ballads, and humorous pieces as well. Their music is thought to have influenced the Protestant Church music which developed later.

The minnesingers, like the troubadours, were of the nobility, and cultivated poetry and song for pure enjoyment and the thrill of accomplishment. They rarely sought the help of jongleurs, as did the troubadours, but themselves sang and played their compositions. The instruments used were viols and lutes—pear-shaped stringed instruments somewhat resembling a mandolin. The viol was played with a bow, the lute by plucking.

Tannhäuser, the chief character in Wagner's great opera of that name, was a minnesinger. Wagner also based the story of his opera *Parsifal* upon a poem written by the minnesinger, Wolfram von Eschenbach. Probably the most famous minnesinger was the talented lyric poet, Walther von der Vogelweide.

The minnesingers gradually disappeared, but a new class of minstrels sprang up, this time among the tradesmen or middle class. They were known as the *meistersingers* (master singers). From the 14th to the 16th centuries they were a prominent part of the musical scene. The meistersingers were well organized into exclusive local societies, and proclaimed themselves as being the only persons competent to set the standards of verse and song. Rigid tests of talent and skill were given to those desiring to join one of their groups. After being accepted, a member was required to pass successfully through several grades before being given the name of *Meister*.

Some groups conducted singing schools, while others held song contests and festivals to spread the art of music. One meistersinger became especially famous as a musical genius. His name was Hans Sachs (died 1576), a humble cobbler who lived in Nuremberg. Wagner's opera "Die Meistersinger von Nürnberg" is based upon the life of this musician.

MUSIC OF THE REFORMATION PERIOD

Invention of Printing

In the middle of the 15th century, Johann Gutenberg invented the process of printing from movable type, which led to the rapid spread of knowledge among the common people. Music was first printed in 1476 by Ulrich Hahn of Rome. Wooden type was used. In 1501, Ottaviano dei Petrucci of Venice printed some books of motets. He did much toward simplifying music notation so that it could be read more easily. At that time notes were square-shaped and music was not divided into measures. When metal replaced wood for the making of type (in the latter part of the 17th century), notes were made oval-shaped like those used today, and bars were used to separate the music into measures.

Martin Luther (1483–1546)

Meanwhile, there arose a movement in Germany which is known as the Reformation of the Church. The leader of the movement was Martin Luther, a former monk of the Catholic Church. We are here particularly interested in Luther only because of what he accomplished for the growth of music. He believed that Church music should be translated from the Latin language into the language which the mass of people understood, and that the people should be given an opportunity to join in the singing. With the help of his friend, Johann Walther, a choir-master and composer, Luther prepared a collection of hymns and chorales, to be used in congregational singing. Some of the melodies were original and some were adapted from popular folk songs. Luther was very fond of music, and played the flute and the lute, but it is doubted by some authorities whether he actually composed. His friend Walther probably contributed the new songs which appeared in his hymn-book. It is well known, however, that Luther wrote the words of most of the hymns. One of the better known is *Ein' feste Burg ist unser Gott*.

At the time when Luther published his hymn-book, the prevailing style of music was contrapuntal, often called polyphonic. That is, the part-writing of that period was based upon counterpoint, and consisted of fitting together two or more melodies so that they sounded in agreement. Counterpoint means literally *note against note*. Luther's chorales and hymns tended to be based upon harmony rather than counterpoint. This means that but one melody was used, supported by an accompaniment of chords or harmony. This style is known as the harmonic style, and became the standard for the composition of Protestant Church music.

Palestrina (1526–1594)

For several years following the death of Pope Gregory, composers of Church music continued to write in the style of the Gregorian Chant. Gradually, however, this music began to lose its artistic qualities; composers corrupted the stately Church music by using secular melodies. Then the words of popular songs were mixed in with the religious texts, until Church music lost its former dignity and sacred character. In 1545 the Church fathers called a meeting, known as the Council of Trent, to discuss, among other matters, means of improving the quality of Church music.

At that time there lived a musician who had drawn much praise for the fine music he had composed. His real name was Giovanni Pierluigi, but he was always known as Palestrina because he was born in the town of that name, near Rome. After the custom followed by artists and musicians of that period, he adopted the name of his birth-place as his own. The council appealed to Palestrina to compose some music which would be worthy of use in Church services. Palestrina immediately set to work and composed three masses, all of them splendid, which were performed before several Cardinals of the Church. One so impressed them with its beauty that it was chosen as a standard for all Church music which should be henceforth composed. It was called the *Mass of Pope Marcellus,* written in honor of a Pope who had helped and encouraged Palestrina in his work.

Some authorities doubt whether Palestrina's part in the revival of Church music was very important, but to this day he is called "the Saviour of Church Music."

THE ORATORIO AND THE OPERA

During the Middle Ages, the priests of the Church found that a very good way to teach the people the Scriptures was to present sacred historical events in the form of plays. These performances were known as moralities, mysteries, or *miracle* plays. To this day, the humble people of Oberammergau, Germany, carry on this custom by acting the Passion Play (a drama of the life of Christ) every ten years.

About 1560, a priest of Rome named Neri conceived the idea of setting to music stories from the Bible, and having them sung after his talks. It became the custom to perform these sacred musical plays in a private room of the Church, called the oratory (from which the word *oratorio* is derived). These plays gained such favor that Neri formed a brotherhood of singers, called the Congregation of the Oratory, whose purpose was to carry on and improve the presentation of the sacred plays. An especially worthy play was written in 1600 by Cavalieri, called *The Representation of the Soul and Body,* which was performed by the brotherhood. Although many similar plays had been presented before this, Cavalieri's play is generally called the first oratorio, because it featured the dramatic solo style, which is a characteristic of the modern oratorio.

A considerable advance in the oratorio was made by Carissimi (1604-1674), born in Marino, near Rome. His work showed unusual imagination and inventiveness; his melodies were free and graceful, and his accompaniments possessed a certain lightness and playfulness. He also greatly improved the *recitative* of the oratorio, and the brilliance and freedom of his writing had a decided influence upon the opera-writing of that period. Carissimi wrote at least fifteen oratorios.

Aside from being a great oratorio-writer, Carissimi developed the *cantata,* which at that time was a short oratorio. Today, cantatas may be secular as well as sacred. The growth of choral societies has been an inducement for composers to write all sorts of cantatas — dramatic, humorous, romantic, fantastic, etc.

The modern oratorio is not really a play at all, because there is no scenery and no acting; the singers merely stand in one position and sing throughout the performance, with an orchestral accompaniment. The singing is performed by a chorus, with solo singers taking the leading parts. The solos of an oratorio are called *recitatives* and *arias.*

Georg Friedrich Handel (1685-1759), stands out as the greatest master of the oratorio. He traveled much, remaining for some time in Italy, where he learned to write oratorios and operas in the Italian style. In 1710, he moved to London. Here his compositions gained great favor with the English people. From 1739, Handel devoted himself almost entirely to the writing and producing of oratorios. He has given us many beautiful melodies which are still popular. Other great composers of oratorios include Haydn, Beethoven, Mendelssohn and Gounod.

Rise of the Opera

Unlike the oratorio, the opera is a real play set to music, in which there is acting, and in which scenery and costumes are used; also, the opera is not necessarily sacred in character. The so-called grand opera almost always contains tragedy.

Toward the end of the 16th century, a group of poets and musicians at Florence, Italy, made efforts to revive the Greek plays, for Greek music and drama had by this time practically disappeared. These artists produced a number of little plays which were set to music, and were known as *monodies*. One of these plays, the music of which was written by two Italians named Peri and Caccini, was called "Dafne." It is commonly known as the first opera.

At this time a young musician named Monteverdi (1567-1643) began to draw attention because of his remarkable genius and originality in musical composition. At the age of sixteen he published a book of madrigals, and it is said that he had learned to play all the instruments which were in use at that time. He was born in Cremona, Italy, but spent most of his life in Venice, devoting himself to the writing of dramatic music. In this he was very successful, and developed the opera far beyond any who had preceded him. He wrote twelve operas, with orchestral accompaniment, but only four of these are in existence. Later he wrote "Ariana" which is considered his best. The orchestral music for these operas calls for the use of more than thirty instruments. The interest which Monteverdi created in the opera caused the first opera house to be built at Venice in 1637.

We have noticed in the case of Church music that without a man of genius to set an example by writing good music, the quality of musical composition deteriorates until some forceful writer with new ideas appears and sets a higher standard. That is what happened to the opera after the influence of Monteverdi and other composers of his time began to decline. Some writers sought to supply a public demand for operas of the comic or burlesque type. Others wrote operas in which the main purpose was to display the technical skill of the singers. The *arias* (solos) were so ornamented and so emphasized at the expense of the plot that the story which the opera was supposed to tell became very obscure.

In the 18th century the opera was reformed by Gluck (1714-1787), a native of Bavaria. He began to write operas which emphasized drama rather than a sensational type of singing. His first opera appeared in 1762, and was based upon the mythological story of Orpheus and Euridice. It marked the beginning of a new style in opera, and possessed the main features of the operas which are heard today.

Many of the great composers since Monteverdi have written operas, but not all were successful and few are heard today. The greatest opera-writer of all time was Richard Wagner (1813-1883), a German composer, who wrote the librettos for his operas as well as the music.

EARLY INSTRUMENTS

In previous chapters little has been said about musical instruments, since we have been discussing for the most part the development of early Church music, which was written entirely for voices. In this brief survey of music history, we shall have to omit many details pertaining to the gradual development of instruments, leaving a more thorough study of the subject to the reader's initiative.

Keyboard Instruments

The first musical instrument to be used in Church services was the organ, which developed from the primitive *hydraulis* previously mentioned. The first organs were of small size such as could be carried from one place to another. In the beginning they were made by monks. Tones were produced by forcing air into pipes of different sizes, the air being released into the various pipes by striking or pressing levers. Bellows, operated by hand, created the air supply, and in the case of larger organs which were built later, several men were required to pump the air into the air chamber. Modern organs get their air supply from a rotary air pump run by electricity. This type of organ is commonly called the *pipe-organ,* and is distinguished from the *reed organ,* which produces tones by means of metal reeds instead of pipes.

The first pipe-organ which is known to have existed in western Europe was presented in 742 by the Emperor Constantine to a ruler of the Frankish Kingdom. In 812, a similar organ was built in Germany, and in 880, the Pope sent for an organ builder from Germany. Keyboards were not invented until the 11th century. From then on keys replaced the clumsy levers of the older instrument.

Early organ music was of the polyphonic style. To the voices of the singers the Church organ was employed as a support or accompaniment only. The most skillful player of the early period was Frescobaldi (1583-1644), an Italian, who was for many years organist at St. Peter's Church in Rome. The man who laid the foundation of modern organ playing and composition was Johann Sebastian Bach (1685-1750). He originated a style which has served ever since as a model for composers and students. Under Bach's influence, the organ tended to become a concert instrument. Our modern pipe-organs, by calling on their tremendous variety of tone-colors and imitations of orchestral instruments, are remarkably capable of simulating a full symphony orchestra.

With the increased use of the organ there arose a demand for small keyboard instruments which could be used in private homes. At first, a type of small portable organ was invented, but it was inconvenient because the player required an assistant to pump the air. Then the idea of building stringed instruments with keyboards was conceived, and from crude beginnings there developed two types of such instruments, the *clavichord* and the *harpsichord.* The clavichord was an oblong box, with strings stretched parallel with the keyboard. It was not supported by legs, but when being played rested upon a table. When a key was struck, a sound was produced from a string by the striking of a little hammer. The tone was very weak, however, and could be heard for only a short distance.

The harpsichord was triangular in shape, somewhat like the modern grand piano. It was much larger than the clavichord, and had legs, although the early models, known as *spinets,* were small table instruments. The sound was produced in a different manner from the clavichord; instead of the strings being struck by hammers, they were plucked with quills, thus giving out a sound similar to that of a harp. The harpsichord was often used in the early orchestras, and it became customary for opera and orchestra conductors to play upon this instrument while conducting.

The tone of the harpsichord, while more brilliant than that of the clavichord, could not be regulated as to loudness and softness. For many years, manufacturers tried in vain to invent a means of overcoming this handicap. In 1711, an Italian harpsichord maker named Cristofori (1655-1731) placed upon exhibition a new type of instrument which became known as the *pianoforte (piano,* soft; *forte,* loud). Its shape was like that of the harpsichord or modern grand piano, and tones were made by the striking of hammers upon strings, but the construction of the instrument was such that both loud and soft tones could be produced by striking the keys with varying degrees of force. Cristofori's mechanical improvement was further developed by other makers, until the pianoforte was firmly established as a practical and superior instrument. The improved construction of the modern pianoforte makes possible a considerable volume of sound. The name of the instrument has been shortened, so that we usually say "piano" instead of "piano-forte." The clavichord and harpsichord were gradually discarded, and by 1800 the piano had become the popular keyboard instrument.

During the last quarter of the 18th century, "square" and "oblong" types of pianos were built. From these, there developed (about 1800) the "upright" type, first introduced by William Southwell.

Stringed Instruments

From now on we shall trace the development of instruments from the 16th century, since from that time the most rapid advance in instrument-making occurred. During the last half of the 16th century the stringed instruments chiefly used were lutes and viols of various sizes. Lutes were played by plucking the strings, while viols were played with bows.

The half of a pear, cut lengthwise, would closely resemble the shape of the lute. The smallest size of lute was called the *chitarra,* and had four strings; the largest, called the *theorbo,* had as many as twenty strings, and was the bass instrument of the lute family.

The word *viol* comes from the German word *fidula* and the Latin *vitula,* from which the English word *fiddle* is derived. Viols were somewhat similar in shape to our violin, but the "shoulders" of the viol were more sloping, the back was flat, and it was strung with five, six, or seven strings. Modern violins, violas, and violoncellos have rounded backs and are strung with four strings. The double bass alone has retained in general the lines of the old viols; it has the sloping shoulders, and many of them in use today have flat backs instead of moulded or rounded backs. There are some five-string double basses being used today in symphony orchestras. Viols were built in five different sizes—treble, alto, tenor, viola-da-gamba, and violone. The first two compare approximately in pitch to our violin; the third, to the modern viola; the fourth, to the violoncello (usually called *cello*), and the fifth to the double bass (often called *bass viol*).

It is uncertain which instrument-maker actually changed the form of the viol into that of the violin, but it may have been Gasparo da Salo, an Italian, who lived during the last half of the 16th century. He was a maker of both viols and violins, and a few of his instruments are still in existence. Ole Bull, the famous Norwegian violinist of the 19th century, owned a genuine Gasparo violin, which is now in a museum in Bergen, Norway.

The names of several famous violin-makers stand out in musical history, most of them Italian. These skilled craftsmen developed the violin to such a high degree of perfection that no one has since been able to make violins which surpass or even equal their instruments in beauty of tone. The old masters of violin-making knew a secret formula for making a varnish which may have in some way contributed to the wonderful tone qualities of their violins. One of the most famous of the early violin-makers was Maggini (1580-1631), a pupil of Gasparo. During the 17th century there lived at Cremona, Italy three noted families of violin-makers: the Amati family, the Guarneri family, and the Stradivari family. The art of violin-making was handed down from father to son, and very often a son would produce much better violins than his father. Jacob Stainer (1621-1683), an Austrian, and a pupil of Amati, made several wonderful violins. He personally chose the wood for his instruments from the forests. It is said that he could tell which trees were of the best quality by tapping them with a hammer. Stainer had difficulty in earning enough to support his large family, and was put in prison for debt. As a result, his health was broken and he died at sixty-two.

The most famous of all violin-makers was Antonio Stradivarius (1644-1737), also a pupil of Amati. He developed his own style of violin, choosing the wood with great care, and taking the utmost pains with every detail of construction. He loved his art, and continued to work in his shop until he was a very old man. It is supposed that Stradivarius made about a thousand violins, and also several cellos and double basses. He sold his violins for one hundred lire (about twenty dollars), but those which are in existence today are valued at several thousand dollars each.

The violin bow, after going through several stages of evolution, was perfected by Francois Tourte of Paris about 1775. The early types of bow were clumsy and rigid, a cord being used instead of the horsehair of modern bows. Tourte's bows were flexible, light, and well-balanced. They made possible the playing of more difficult music, and marked the beginning of a new era in violin-playing.

Wind Instruments

During the period of the 16th to the 18th centuries, it was customary to make most kinds of wind instruments in several sizes, just as were the lutes and viols of the string class.

There were two kinds of flute in use, the vertical and the transverse flute. The first type was played by blowing air through a mouthpiece at the end of the instrument. The transverse flute was played by holding the instrument in a horizontal position and blowing against the edge of a hole near the end of the tube. This is the type used today.

The ancestor of the modern oboe, English horn, and bassoon was the *shawm*. It was played by blowing air through a double reed inserted in the end of a wooden tube having finger holes.

The trumpet was at first a long straight tube of metal. Later, it was coiled upon itself for convenience in playing. Sections of tubing in various sizes, called crooks or shanks, could be inserted in the instrument so that it could be played in different keys. The trumpet was called the *tromba* during the 18th century, and this name will be found in many orchestral scores in use today.

The forerunner of the modern cornet was the *cornett.* The early type was made of wood, having a cupped mouthpiece and usually seven holes for the fingers. The bass member of the cornett family was the *serpent,* a long S-shaped tube of wood.

The *sackbut* was a high-pitched or treble-trombone about the size of a trumpet, and appeared about the 14th century. It had a U-shaped slide, which could be pushed in and out to play different tones.

The *corno* was a horn resembling the modern French horn. It appeared during the latter part of the 17th century and became common after 1750. The corno developed from the hunting horn, and was made of twelve or more feet of metal tubing bent in a circular form. Crooks could be inserted to change the pitch of the instrument.

The *chalumeau,* ancestor of the clarinet, was invented about 1700. It was a tube of wood with finger holes, and was blown through a mouthpiece having a single reed.

THE CLASSICAL PERIOD

The musical development of the 18th century is generally referred to as the classical period, and began with the works of Johann Sebastian Bach (1685-1750) and Georg Friedrich Handel (1685-1759). Bach, who became famous as a composer and organist, is known as the greatest master of polyphonic music, a style of writing which prevailed during the 15th and 16th centuries. Handel is known as the greatest writer of oratorios.

Under the leadership of Bach and Handel, music of the period took on new and improved forms. The fugue, a favorite form of composition with both composers, provided a means for greater artistic expression, more effective contrasts, and greater freedom for display of original ideas than any of the forms previously used.

Bach had several sons who possessed talent for music. One of them, Karl Philipp Emanuel Bach (1714-1788), became an excellent clavier player, and founded a style of musical composition which set new standards for other composers to follow. He is given credit for the founding of the sonata-form, which was later perfected by Franz Joseph Haydn (1732-1809).

Haydn adopted the homophonic (also called monophonic) style of composition, basing his work upon patterns established by K. P. E. Bach. He confined his compositions to a strict form, which is a characteristic of the music of the "classical" period. Haydn used the sonata form in writing for the orchestra, and he thereby established the *symphony*, a word which signifies a sonata for orchestra. To this day, Haydn is called "the father of the symphony."

The next great musician to contribute to the development of music was Wolfgang Amadeus Mozart (1756-1791), one of the foremost geniuses in musical history. Using the same precise form of composition employed by Haydn, he gave to his melodies and harmonies a beauty and charm that placed his works upon a higher plane than those of Haydn. His operas contained more vitality and showed a better handling of dramatic situations than the operas of Gluck. Mozart set standards which later inspired Beethoven to attain great heights in the field of composition.

The word "classic" refers not so much to this period of musical history, as it does to the kind of music then written. Two characteristics of this music might well be mentioned. In the first place, it means music which is written in some certain form, and which does not deviate from that form. For example, an early composer of the period might write several compositions, and give them a name significant to him because it described what he was trying to do. Another composer who admired his predecessor's work, would write in the same form, and call it by the same name chosen by the first composer. Thus we have such well established forms as *motet, sonata, concerto, suite, chaconne, toccata, fugue, prelude,* and *rondo*. Another characteristic of classic music is the emphasis on the music itself. This can best be described through the uses of the terms program and absolute music. Program music is music which describes something. It is sometimes called descriptive music. Absolute music, on the other hand, is music which is *pure,* constructed on the basis of the form in which it was written, and not intended to describe.

THE ROMANTIC PERIOD

The romantic movement originated in Germany, and represented a tendency toward greater imagination and fuller musical expression. Musical ideals were changing rapidly during the latter part of the 18th century. It was plain that new forms of composition were needed through which composers could not only impart a sense of beauty, but could tell a story or express their inmost feelings through the medium of music. They found the forms established by the Viennese classical school too rigid for this purpose.

With the advent of Ludwig van Beethoven (1770-1827), a new era in instrumental music was opened. Beethoven's early works show the influence of Haydn and Mozart, but his later compositions reveal a marked tendency to break through the boundaries of formalism set by the classical school. He enlarged the sonata-form, and developed the symphony to proportions that were far more ambitious than the works of his predecessors. He was gifted with remarkable inventiveness and imagination, and his works pointed the way toward still more radical changes which were to take place later.

Franz Peter Schubert (1797-1828), a Viennese composer, was a great admirer of Beethoven, and received much inspiration from the study of his works. Schubert was a song-writer at heart, and is famous for his devotion to the composition of artistic songs (art songs). He wrote much instrumental music also, but the lyric qualities of the song are always in evidence. One needs but to listen to his immortal "Unfinished Symphony" to observe his gift for melody. He made no radical departure from the classical style, but he wrote in a free and spontaneous manner, revealing a deep imagination and a remarkable musical instinct.

The German opera felt the influence of the romantic movement through the work of Carl Maria von Weber (1786-1826). Because of his bold leadership in music reform, Weber is frequently called the founder of the romantic movement. This honor might well be shared, however, with Robert Schumann (1810-1856), an eminent composer of the 19th century.

Schumann became editor of a musical journal in Leipzig, and through its columns he openly criticized the restricting influence of the classical school, and proclaimed that a new movement was under way. One of his favorite forms was the *Fantasia,* a type of composition which has no special plan, and which allows the composer's imagination a free rein.

Felix Mendelssohn-Bartholdy (1809-1847) lived during the period of romanticism, but he seems never to have been entirely in sympathy with the radical changes which were taking place in musical composition. He was a genius with fresh ideas, but he tended to cling more or less to the forms of the classical school.

The spirit of the romantic movement prevails in the works of Frederic Chopin (1810-1849), a Polish pianist and composer. He devoted almost his entire attention to composition for the piano, and is reckoned as the foremost composer for that instrument. He is often called "The Poet of the Piano."

Hector Berlioz (1803-1869) stands out as one of the most dominating figures in the development of instrumental music. His tendency was to compose in large dimensions. His grandiose ideas are manifested in his orchestral numbers, which call for orchestras of huge proportions. The score for his "Tuba Mirum" demands two piccolos, four flutes, four clarinets, eight oboes, twelve horns, a full choir of strings, sixteen trumpets, sixteen trombones, two tubas, and four ophicleides (now obsolete). Such radical instrumentation had been unheard of before Berlioz, but his works furnished ideas for later composers, even though they did not follow him to such extremes.

New standards were set in the realm of piano virtuosity by the Hungarian pianist and composer, Franz Liszt (1811-1866). His inventiveness and genius for original effects, contrasts, and tone color won him a place of high rank as a composer for both piano and orchestra. His ability as a concert pianist was unmatched in his day.

Richard Wagner (1813-1883) is known as the greatest opera composer of all time. Through his efforts, the opera rose to a definitely higher plane. Wagner's vocal scores made such great demands upon the technique of singers, and his orchestral accompaniments were considered so sensational that his music was not readily accepted during his early career. His aim was to create unity between the text and the music of his operas, asserting that the music should aid in expressing the dramatic situations of the play. He was very persistent in his efforts to carry out his ideas, and to a great extent succeeded in overcoming popular prejudice. Wagner's genius is fully recognized today, and his operas are considered artistic masterpieces.

The works of Peter Ilyitch Tschaikowsky (1840-1893), Russian composer, also abound with the spirit of romanticism. One of the chief features of his symphonies is the passing from one mood to another several times—from gayety to melancholy, or from noisy boisterousness to tender sentiment.

The last composer to be mentioned in connection with the romantic period is Johannes Brahms (1833-1897), an eminent German pianist and composer. The world's estimate of his scholarly symphonies and other works place him in musical history as the logical successor to Beethoven. Brahms was a conservative in respect to form, but his genius for beautiful melody, unique harmonies, and emotional expression places him within the romantic period.

The romantic period, then, may best be described as a time of breaking away from traditional formalism, letting fancy run free, and establishing new forms of composition. From many viewpoints, it is the most important period in musical history, because it furnished the basis for our modern music. Probably more music from the romantic period is played today than from any other musical era.

MODERN MUSIC

It is impossible to draw any definite dividing line between the romantic and the modern in musical history. It would be inaccurate to say that modern music dates from the beginning of the twentieth century, because modern tendencies were taking root long before that time. We might say that Berlioz and Wagner were modernists, although their careers ended several years before the end of the 19th century. The fact is, that their ideas were so far in advance of the prevailing styles of their time, that there may well arise the question whether to identify them as extreme romanticists or pioneer modernists.

Richard Strauss (1864) is sometimes called the last German composer of the romantic movement, but at least a portion of his works have their place in the modern period of music. Of his works, his symphonic poems have gained the most acceptance, these appearing frequently on symphony concert programs. A spirit of restlessness and turbulence dominates much of his work. Strauss is known as a *realist*. He aims to portray through his music various sides of modern civilization.

Jean Sibelius (1865), a living Finnish composer, is representative of the modern school of symphonists. He is an experimenter, and has introduced entirely new principles of form into his symphonies. His musical expression tends toward weirdness and mystery.

Impressionism represents a type of music which is characteristically modern. It is concerned with pictorial effects—the painting of musical pictures. Traditional rules of harmony are disregarded if they interfere with the composer's purpose. The pioneer impressionist was the French composer, Claude Debussy (1862-1918). Maurice Ravel (1875) is a famous living French impressionist. The Russian school of impressionism is represented by Alexander Scriabin (1872-1915).

Ernest Bloch (1880), a Jewish Swiss composer, is one of the most talented living impressionists. He came to America in 1916, thereafter exerting considerable influence on young American composers. In 1930 his composition "America" won a prize. In this work he attempts to convey his impressions of his adopted country, devoting a section to typical American jazz music. Other compositions include symphonies, symphonic poems, a string quartet, the operas "Macbeth" and "Jezebel" (unfinished), and other works.

John Alden Carpenter (1876) should be mentioned as one of the outstanding modern American composers. His works include the orchestral suite "Adventures in a Perambulator," the ballet "Skyscrapers," a violin sonata, a "Concertino" for piano and orchestra, and several songs.

One of the most radical innovators of the modern period is Igor Stravinsky (1882), a Russian composer. His aim has been to develop a style which would be definitely his own, and for his purpose he studied the works of the 18th century masters, calling himself a *classicist.* He is also known as a *futurist* and an *ultra-modernist.*

Deems Taylor (1885) is a famous living American impressionist who has been remarkably successful in the field of the modern opera. His "Peter Ibbetson" and "The King's Henchman" have been performed at the Metropolitan Opera House in New York. His suite for orchestra, "Through the Looking Glass," has met with popular acclaim, and his symphonic poem, "The Siren Song," won a prize in 1913.

Jazz is considered by Europeans to be the typical modern music of America. It is true that many of our outstanding modern American composers have introduced jazz rhythms into their works in their efforts to identify them as typically American. The principal feature of jazz is syncopation—the retarding and anticipating of harmony and melody. The style originated with the Negro, and the white man has imitated it.

Some composers have developed jazz into an art. Among the most prominent of these are George Gershwin, who wrote "Rhapsody in Blue"; Ferde Grofé, composer of "Grand Canyon Suite" and "Metropolis"; and Werner Janssen, composer of "New Year's Eve in New York."

[For selected references for Chapter III see page 139]

CHAPTER IV

MUSICAL FORM

"How sour sweet music is when time is broke and no proportion kept."

SHAKESPEARE'S RICHARD II

LET US suppose that we wish to erect a building. Our first step is probably the selection of an architect to draw plans for the building according to the purpose for which the building is to be used. Suppose again that we wish to save money and decide to omit the architect. We hire a contractor and tell him to buy the materials and erect a building. Suppose again that the contractor knows nothing about architecture and erects a bungalow with a church spire. Such a structure does not fit the accepted style for bungalows. To put it in the mildest way our building is deficient in *form.* The same unhappy situation would result if we were to write music without form. Form may best be described as the structure, design, or plan of the music. In literature is found perhaps the best analogy. Let us, for example, divide literature into poems, short stories, books, and serials. Within each division there are smaller units. A poem is made up of lines and stanzas; a book is separated into chapters. In other words, there is a well developed plan or form by which the work is organized and completed. To carry our literary analogy a step further, compare the nomenclature of literature and music:

LITERATURE	MUSIC
letter	note
syllable	figure
word	motive
phrase	phrase
sentence	period
paragraph	section
chapter	movement
story	composition

The reason many readers find Gertrude Stein confusing and meaningless is that she quite ignores accepted rules of writing and offers us her own instead. Music, if it is to be comprehensible, must necessarily adhere even more closely to familiar rules governing its plan and structure. Like literature, it has numerous forms, so that the composer is not limited in his endeavors. If, for example, we desire to write a short piece for piano, we have many choices. We may write an etude, a prelude, a nocturne, a rhapsody, or another of the great number of such forms. If we wish to write in a more ambitious manner we might choose the sonata, concerto, or the symphony. After we have chosen our form, we adhere to the rules that govern its design. Different rules exist for the different forms.

A knowledge of the essentials of all musical forms must of course be reserved for the student of music, since the rules are so varied for each form, and the forms so numerous that it takes much study and experimentation to be able to use them all. For all people who wish merely to listen to music, however, it is extremely valuable to be able to distinguish between the various smaller forms. Therefore brief descriptions of some of these will be given.

Musical form may be defined as the design or plan of a composition, in which the principles of unity, variety, and sequence are observed.

A series of musical thoughts or sentences is composed to fit the design of a song. There are usually at least two distinct sections. These sections or phrases may be likened to questions and answers. The phrase representing the question is known as the antecedent. The answering phrase is called the consequent. They are also known as *thesis* and *antithesis*, respectively. For convenience in analyzing compositions, phrases are designated by letter names: A-B-C, etc. Usually at least one of them is repeated somewhere in the composition. The repetition is sometimes an exact one, and sometimes differs slightly from the original. Thus, if section A is repeated exactly, we designate the repetition by another A. If the repetition is slightly changed, it is indicated by A′.

The *Unitary* form consists of only one section, and is rarely found. Compositions of this form are so brief that they require no division into sections.

The *Binary* form is composed of two sections, usually of eight measures each. Nearly all simple folk songs are of this form, and generally contain repetition. The example below illustrates one type of the Binary form, the A-A-B-A form. This song contains two distinct sections, with a repetition of the first part (phrase A) occurring twice. The first half-phrase represents the question; the half-phrase immediately following represents the answer. Phrase B is an entirely different melody, returning to the original in the final phrase.

DRINK TO ME ONLY WITH THINE EYES

Another type of the Binary form is the A-A′-B-A′ form. The appearance of A′ indicates a repetition which differs slightly from the original phrase. The following example illustrates this form.

Note that the difference between phrases A and A′ is in the cadences, which occur in the last two measures of each phrase. The first cadence is the progression $\text{I-}\overset{7}{V}_1$; the second is $\overset{7}{V}_1\text{-I}$.

LIGHTLY ROW

The *Ternary* form consists of three distinct sections (A-B-C), illustrated in the following example:

SILENT NIGHT, HOLY NIGHT

CHARACTERISTIC STYLES AND FORMS

Having learned to distinguish the various parts of the simple musical forms, the student should become acquainted with different styles or types of composition. The proper classification of a composition may generally be determined by its rhythmic, harmonic, and melodic qualities.

There are, however, three other elements of form which must be considered before a composition may be definitely assigned to a classification. They are unity, variety, and sequence. Unity may be defined as the consistency of a composition; the tendency to follow the general rules which apply to each form or style. Variety, of course, is the tendency to deviate from the monotony of rigid adherence to initial style. Sequence, which is the repetition of melody units either on the same pitch, or higher or lower in the scale, is an aid to both unity and variety. Below are described some of the many forms in which music may be written, with the characteristics that distinguish each.

Anthem

The term is usually applied to religious texts set to music, to be sung by a choir as part of a Protestant church service. There are also anthems of rejoicing and national anthems. The form of the anthem is somewhat the same as that of the motet, but modern practice permits many variations.

Ballad

The *ballad* was originally a dance-song, but the term was later used in connection with any folk-like song that told a story. The sentiment expressed may be amorous, religious, comic, satirical, etc. During the period of Schubert and the rise of the art-song, the term came to mean a dramatic song. From the 19th century, any compositions for piano, orchestra, and choir were called ballads, or *ballades*. They usually contain verses and repeated choruses, or refrains.

Ballet

The term originated near the end of the 16th century, and was applied to part-songs or madrigals of a gay nature, written in the style of dance-tunes. In France, during the 17th century, the term was applied to dance-pageants presented upon the stage with musical accompaniment. In the early 19th century, the ballet came to be an independent entertainment in connection with grand opera, often having no connection with the plot of the opera. The name ballet was applied to either the dance-spectacle itself, or to the group of dancers. It is now used in connection with independent dance-presentations.

Barcarolle

The *barcarolle* is usually written in $\frac{6}{8}$ meter, and is played at a moderate tempo. The accompaniment, the distinguishing characteristic of the barcarolle, simulates the motion of a boat rocking upon the waves. The melody is of a lyric style and suggests the singing of a gondolier.

Berceuse

Berceuse is the French name for cradle song, or lullaby. It may be written in triple or in quadruple meter; the movement is moderately slow. The motion of a rocking cradle is suggested by the accompaniment, and the melody represents the song of the mother.

Canon

The *canon* is a form of composition in which a theme given by a leading voice part is imitated exactly, note for note, either at the same or on a different pitch, by another voice part which begins a few beats after the first. The leading voice part is sometimes called the antecedent, and the imitating part the consequent. The canon may have an ending called a coda, or it may lead back to the beginning and continue indefinitely. It is the strictest form of contrapuntal composition. The name is derived from *canone,* meaning rule, or law.

Carol

The *carol* is of English origin, and is usually associated with Christmas or Easter. It differs from the hymn in being of a ballad-like style, and often containing a fanciful or jocular text. Christmas carols are also known as noëls.

Chorale

The *chorale* has its origin in Protestant church music. The style was in imitation of existing secular songs of metrical stanza-form. The melody was written in the tenor until the latter part of the 16th century, when it was gradually transferred to the soprano. From the 17th century it became customary to use notes mostly of the same length, producing a smooth, even rhythm. A long note, or a pause, usually occurs at the end of each phrase.

Concerto

The *concerto* is an elaborate sonata for a solo instrument, with an orchestral accompaniment. It usually consists of three movements.

Descant

The *descant* is an early form of contrapuntal composition in which a high voice sings a separate, or counter melody in harmony with and above the other parts. The added voice part is also called the descant. This form has recently been revived for modern use and has become quite popular.

Etude

The *etude* was originally a study, written for the display of technique. The harmonic qualities, as a rule, are made prominent, while the melodic elements are obscured in the background. However, some composers, such as Chopin and Rubinstein, have written etudes that are artistic and interesting, the technical devices giving way to lyrical qualities.

Folk Music

Folk music includes both folk songs and folk dances, which have originated and become traditional among the common people or peasant class. A folk tune is not always identified with any particular composer, but may be handed down orally from one generation to the next. It expresses sentiment that is typical of the community in which it originated, and is usually in ballad form.

Fugue

The *fugue,* like the *canon,* is a contrapuntal form best identified by the use of thematic imitation. That is, a subject is introduced by one part or voice, and is answered or imitated, by other parts. Unlike the canon, however, the fugue need not be in strict imitation, but may be varied in melodic direction. If the fugue is written in two voices, it is called a two-voiced fugue; if in three, a three-voiced fugue, etc. If there are two themes, it is called a double fugue. It derives its name from the Latin word *fuga,* meaning *flight.*

Glee

Originally a part-song for three or more voices without accompaniment, which developed in England about 1700. The *glee* is broken up into several brief strains or phrases, and contains interesting figures and patterns. It differs from the madrigal and motet in being in the modern major or minor mode. The spirit of the glee is not necessarily cheerful or jocular, as its name implies, but may be serious or even sad. The term Glee Club is derived from the glee.

Hunting Song

Most *hunting songs* contain groups of notes intended to imitate the hunting horn. They are usually in $\frac{6}{8}$ meter, and in lively tempo.

Hymn

A religious poem set to music. The bards of ancient Greece sang and played hymns (also known as odes) to their deities. The *hymn* as we know it today is designed for choir and congregational singing in connection with Christian worship.

Intermezzo

The term *intermezzo* was originally applied to a piece performed between the acts of a play or an opera. In the 16th century, songs in madrigal style, accompanied by instruments, usually served as intermezzi. From these the intermezzo developed into a complete musical play or humorous drama, used for entertainment between the acts of a serious opera. Its increasing popularity gave rise to the Opera Buffa, an independent comic opera. The term intermezzo is also applied to an extra movement inserted in an instrumental suite, sonata, or symphony.

Invention

The *invention* is much the same as the etude. It is a short piano piece containing technical material for the music student. It is usually written in contrapuntal style and in two, three, or four parts.

Madrigal

The *madrigal* originated in Flanders in the 15th century, and is closely related to the Motet. It is a lyrical song in one of the medieval modes, written for three or more voices, unaccompanied. Madrigals were often used as intermezzi in the early operas and oratorios, but from about 1625 other forms gradually took their place. In recent years, interest in the madrigal has been revived, and has led to the organization of societies whose purpose has been to encourage the composition and performance of madrigals.

Mass

Mass is the name for a service in the Catholic church, part of which is read with the speaking voice by the church dignitaries, and part of which is sung by the choir at certain points. The part performed by the choir constitutes the musical *mass,* with which we are here concerned. It ordinarily consists of six principal divisions, as follows: the Kyrie, the Gloria, the Credo, the Sanctus, the Benedictus, and the Agnus Dei.

Motet

The term *motet* originated in France about the 13th century, and applied to secular part-songs, written in the medieval modes. In three-part songs, the middle voice was called the *motetus;* hence the name, motet. From the 15th century, Biblical texts set to music, and designed for several voices without accompaniment, were called motets. During the 18th century, the style of the motet became varied until it became practically the same as an English anthem. Motets are usually distinguished by having Latin texts, or by the lack of any accompaniment.

Nocturne

The *nocturne* is of a dreamy, sentimental nature, written in a lyrical style. It is closely related to the serenade and romance. The term *nocturne* means *night song.*

Overture

The *overture* serves the same purpose as the prelude. It is used as an introduction to an opera, oratorio, and cantata, and usually contains excerpts from the work which it introduces. Like the prelude, the term is often applied to independent compositions. The formal overture was developed by Lully in France during the latter part of the 17th century. His type of overture consisted of three movements: the first, slow; the second, fast; and the third, a slow dance, such as the minuet. Later, the overture came to be written in one movement, divided into contrasting sections of fast and slow tempi. The term *overture* means *beginning.*

Prelude

An instrumental piece of any kind, used as an introduction for what is to follow. It may serve as an introductory movement to a fugue, or as an instrumental introduction to an opera or to any choral work. The term is also applied to an organ number played at the beginning of a church service. Chopin and other composers have given this title to independent compositions.

Rhapsody

The *rhapsody* is an instrumental fantasia. The form is often extremely irregular, disconnected, and fantastic. Liszt introduced this form of composition, using national melodies and folk tunes as a basis.

Rondo

The *rondo* is an instrumental composition best described by its recurring principal theme. This theme usually occurs at least three times, and is separated from each recurrence by a contrasting theme. The term *rondo* means literally *round*, but this form should not be confused with the *round* which is a much more simple form. Unity in the rondo is secured by the recurrent principal theme, and variety by the contrasting theme.

Round

The *round* is a species of canon, differing from the canon in that the imitating voice parts enter in unison with the leading part and at regular rhythmic intervals. The round in addition, has no ending but continues indefinitely.

Scherzo

The *scherzo* is a type of composition which suggests humor or playfulness. Beethoven introduced this form into his sonatas and symphonies, in place of the older minuet (as used by Haydn). The scherzo is written in triple meter; the tempo is bright and rapid. Many scherzi by Beethoven or Mendelssohn, written for orchestra, may be played upon the piano.

Sonata

The *sonata* is an elaborate composition in three or four movements, written for a solo instrument, such as the violin, piano, or cello. It originated from the older *suite*. Sonatas for the chamber-music groups are called trios, quartets, quintets, etc.

Spiritual

Spirituals constitute a type of American folk music, having originated among the negroes during the period of slavery in the South. They reflect the religious fervor which prevailed on plantations and at camp meetings.

Symphony

The *symphony* is an enlarged form of the sonata, written for orchestra. It originally consisted of three movements, but later a fourth movement was added. The movements of the modern symphony usually, but not always, consist of the following: First movement — Allegro, often preceded by a slow introduction, and usually in sonata form. Second movement — Andante, containing thematic material expressing lofty sentiment. Third movement — a Scherzo, suggesting playfulness or humor. Last movement — a fast tempo, such as Allegro, or Allegro Vivace.

DANCE FORMS

Gavotte

The *gavotte* is an old French dance originating in the 16th century. It is written in duple meter, with a moderate tempo, and a steady and even rhythm. It always begins on the last half of a measure.

March (Funeral)

The *funeral march* is a slow stately march intended as a dirge for the dead. It is always in duple meter, and with a slow and solemn tempo.

March (Military)

The *military march* is a quick, lively composition, intended originally as an accompaniment for marching. Modern usage permits the use of marches in concert programs, especially for bands. It is in duple meter, and has a marching tempo.

March (Processional)

The *processional march* has the same meter and rhythm as the military march but the tempo is much more stately and much slower. It is intended as an accompaniment for processions, and is usually used at weddings, commencement exercises, and for state occasions.

Mazurka

The *mazurka* is of Polish origin. It is written in triple meter, with a moderately slow tempo. It can best be described by its constant contrast of a smooth, flowing rhythm to a characteristic jerky rhythm. An accent usually occurs on the *second* beat of each measure.

Minuet

The *minuet* is an old French court dance. It is written in triple meter, with a moderately slow tempo, and a slight accent on the third beat of the measure. In early symphonies, the minuet constituted the final movement; in later symphonies, the third movement. Beethoven, in his symphonies, replaced the minuet with the *scherzo*.

Polka

The *polka* is a dance of Bohemian origin, in duple meter, and written in a rather fast tempo. The characteristic polka has an accent on the first three eighth-note beats of each measure.

Polonaise

The *polonaise* is a Polish court dance, originating about the 16th century. It is written in triple meter, and usually in a slow tempo. It possesses a stately character that suggests a procession. This dance has been idealized by Chopin.

Schottische

The *schottische* is a variation of the polka. It is written in duple meter, and has a tempo somewhat slower than a march.

Tango

The *tango* is a Mexican dance, closely related to the *Habanera* (a Cuban dance) but with a livelier tempo. It is written in duple meter.

Waltz (Classic)

The classic *waltz* has the same meter as the common waltz (triple), but the tempo is too fast for dancing. Its general character is often brilliant and sometimes fantastic.

Waltz (Common)

The common *waltz*, better known as the modern ballroom waltz, is in triple meter, and has a graceful, flowing rhythm. The old German ballroom waltz consisted of a series of waltzes joined together, usually preceded by a slow introduction.

[For selected references for Chapter IV see page 139]

CHAPTER V

MUSICAL INSTRUMENTS

"It is the nature of instrumental music in its highest form to express in sounds what is inexpressible in words."

RICHARD WAGNER

INSTRUMENTAL music is probably as old as music itself. Did you know that King David was an instrumentalist? Biblical history records the fact that he played two instruments, and that he was an accomplished performer on both of them. Constantly employed by Nebuchadnezzar was a court band of instrumentalists playing string, brass, and percussion instruments. Moses was given precise instructions in the making of trumpets: "Make thee two trumpets of silver, of a whole piece shalt thou make them, that thou mayst use them for the calling of the assembly. With trumpet and sound of cymbals make a joyful noise unto the Lord thy King."

Since there are only two means of musical expression, vocal and instrumental, the instruments themselves assume a role of major importance in our musical system. Not only is each instrument important in itself, but more important still, is the combination of instruments into groups. These groups vary in nature according to the number of instruments, the purpose for which they are formed, and the particular variety and proportion of instruments used. For example, a string quartet is intended for use in a small hall or auditorium, whence arose the term *chamber music.* It is composed of only four instruments: two violins, a viola, and a violoncello; hence the term *quartet.* The symphony orchestra on the other hand, is intended for a large auditorium, uses all of the orchestral instruments, with a specific proportion according to the size of the orchestra, but sets no limit on the total number of instruments used. The band employs somewhat the same proportions as the orchestra but does not use the stringed instruments, and adds the baritone or euphonium, the saxophone, E-flat alto, and alto clarinet. Although the scores do not provide for it, modern bands do sometimes use the double bass, and in some instances even cellos have been included.

It would be difficult to say which is the most important, the band or the orchestra. Certainly the band is more widely heard. Whoever heard of a circus, or a parade, or an army without a band? Why is it that the band leads the procession? Shrewd politicians know that a band engenders enthusiasm and that it draws crowds to hear their speakers. The crowd always follows the band. The term *band* comes to us from the French word *bande*, meaning a group of instruments. Today, however, the band means much more than that; and we have developed several different kinds of bands. The full military band which accompanies the army on its marches, the brass band which was developed for use with cavalry and leaves out the reed instruments, and the concert band with which we are so well acquainted, all have their definite places in our social and musical life. Few communities indeed are there which do not have their municipal concert bands. In fact, the popularity and number of these bands has increased so rapidly during recent years that some states have enacted laws assessing taxes for their support.

The orchestra has likewise been a potent influence in our music. It is said that in symphonic music our composers reach the height of their achievement. At least it it true that some of our greatest music has been written for the symphony orchestra. Not only is the orchestra capable of stirring our deepest emotions, but like the paintings of the great masters, represents the height of our artistic and cultural attainments.

Instrumental music has not always had a pleasant and uneventful existence. Our Puritan forefathers for example, acquired a prejudice against the use of music in the church. They banished all musical instruments as being "instruments of the devil." Today, however, almost all schools give to the pupils who so desire, an opportunity to play instruments in the school band or orchestra. The instruments which make up these organizations will therefore be described in some detail, in the hope that the knowledge may intrigue the reader to such an extent that he may wish to know the thrill of playing one of them.

INSTRUMENTS OF THE MODERN ORCHESTRA AND BAND

The word *orchestra* may be defined as a group of instruments and players, in which the stringed instruments are the most prominent.

The strings (violins, violas, 'cellos, and double basses) greatly outnumber the wind instruments, and provide the characteristic tone color of the orchestra. A small orchestra of about fifteen players would likely consist of two or three first violins, one or two second violins, one viola, one 'cello, one double bass, one flute, one clarinet, one cornet, one trombone, a bass drum, snare drum, some small percussion instruments, perhaps two kettledrums (tympani), and a piano. If such an orchestra were to be enlarged, strings would be added in greater proportion than wind instruments, and the piano would eventually be discarded.

A symphony orchestra is composed of from fifty to one hundred or more expert players. It has a correct balance of strings and winds, and is capable of playing the great masterpieces of musical literature in an artistic manner.

Instruments are divided into three general classes or families: strings, winds, and percussion. These groups may be subdivided as follows:

Minneapolis Symphony Orchestra

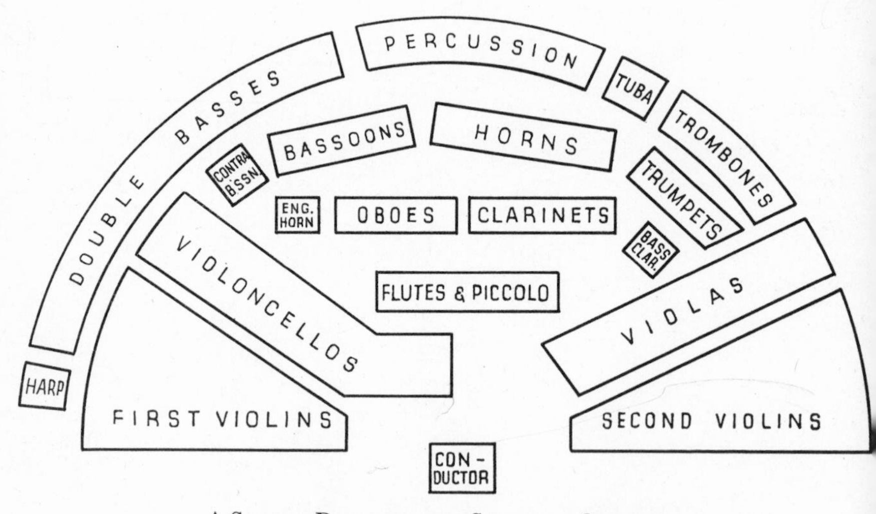

A Seating Diagram for a Symphony Orchestra

(Compare with the seating arrangement of the Minneapolis Symphony Orchestra shown above.)

I. STRINGED INSTRUMENTS

(a) INSTRUMENTS PLAYED WITH A BOW:

Violin
Viola
Violoncello ('cello)
Double bass

(b) INSTRUMENTS PLAYED BY PLUCKING THE STRINGS:

Harp
Guitar, *Mandolin*, *Banjo* — *Rarely used in orchestras.*

II. WIND INSTRUMENTS

(a) WOOD-WINDS:

Piccolo, *Flute* — *Sounded by blowing across a hole near the end of tube.*
Oboe, *English horn*, *Bassoon*, *Contra bassoon* — *Double reed instruments.*
Clarinet, *Alto clarinet*, *Bass clarinet*, *Saxophone* — *Single reed instruments.*

(b) BRASS-WINDS (INSTRUMENTS WITH CUPPED MOUTHPIECES):

Trumpet
Cornet
French horn
Trombone
Tuba
Alto horn
Mellophone
Baritone
Euphonium

III. PERCUSSION INSTRUMENTS

Kettledrums (Tympani)
Side drum (Snare drum)
Bass drum
Tambourine
Cymbals
Triangle
Castanets
Gong
Glockenspiel (bells)

In a large symphony orchestra (ninety to one hundred or more players), the approximate proportion of instruments would be as follows:

16 or 18 1st violins
14 or 16 2nd violins
12 or 14 violas
10 or 12 violoncellos
8 or 10 double basses
1 harp
3 flutes
1 piccolo
3 oboes
1 English horn
3 bassoons
1 contra bassoon
3 clarinets
1 bass clarinet
4 French horns
3 or 4 trumpets
3 trombones
1 tuba
3 or 4 kettledrums
1 side drum
1 bass drum
Bells, cymbals, triangle, and other percussion instruments.

Some composers have included in their scores such instruments as E-flat clarinet, E-flat trumpet, saxophone, guitar, piano, and celesta (a keyboard instrument giving a mellow, bell-like sound). These instruments, when called for, are usually played by some of the regular players in the orchestra who "double;" so-called because the players have ability to play two or more instruments. Sometimes, when a particular composition calls for rarely used instruments, it is necessary to engage extra players.

Again, some composers have written music calling for more than the usual number of instruments used in the orchestra. Wagner's "Die Walküre" calls for six harps, two piccolos, eight horns, a bass trumpet, and four trombones, besides the full number of other instruments. Berlioz was the originator of large orchestras with unusual instrumentation. Among his works are found scores calling for twelve horns, sixteen trumpets, sixteen trombones, sixteen kettledrums, two bass drums, etc.

On the other hand, many compositions require only a part of the usual variety of instruments. Mozart wrote some charming music for strings only. Beethoven, in his Fifth Symphony, wrote for two horns instead of four, and omitted the bass clarinet and tuba.

Various symphony orchestras have their own seating plans, which are decided by the individual conductors. The players are always seated so that they form a semi-circle in front of the conductor, and can watch the movements of his baton. The first violins are invariably seated at the left of the conductor, at the front of the stage. The principal player of the first violin section is called the *concertmaster.* He sits at the first desk of that section. The violin player on his left is called the assistant concertmaster.

Probably the most common seating plan is to have the first violins at the left front of the stage, the second violins at the right front, the 'cello section just behind the first violins, and the viola section behind the second violins.

The wood-winds are located directly in front of the conductor; the horns are behind the wood-winds. At the left rear of the stage are the double basses. Kettledrums are at the rear center, and just to the right of them, the other percussion instruments. At the right rear of the stage are the tuba and trombones; in front of them, the trumpets. The harp is placed in various positions, depending upon the wish of the conductor.*

The following paragraphs describe briefly the various instruments of the symphony orchestra:

STRINGED INSTRUMENTS

The Violin

The violin is the soprano member of the string choir. It is the smallest of the stringed instruments, and its tone is the most brilliant and penetrating. It has four strings, tuned E-A-D-G, as follows:

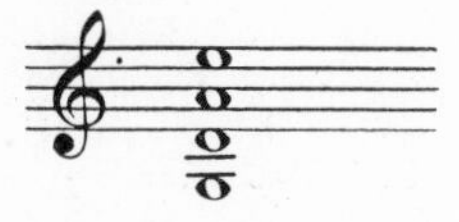

The first violins are required to play the greater part of the leading themes or melodies of a composition, although they are often assigned to play counter-melody parts against other instruments.

The second violins usually play a part that corresponds to the alto part in choral music, although they are often used to reinforce the first violins in their part, or to play a counter-melody.

The Viola

The viola has the same appearance as the violin at a distance, but upon closer inspection it will be found

* See page 81 for seating diagram.

to be slightly larger than the violin. Its tone is not so brilliant, but is full and rich. Most music for the viola is written in the alto clef, although temporary shifts to the treble clef are occasionally made for passages containing high notes.

The four strings of the viola are tuned A-D-G-C, as follows:

The part taken by the violas generally corresponds to the tenor part in choral music, but they are used in various other ways also. They frequently play the melody with some other instrument.

The Violoncello ('cello)

The violoncello is the bass member of the string choir. Its four strings have the same names as those of the viola (A-D-G-C), but are tuned one octave lower, as follows:

The 'cello is held between the knees of the player, the neck of the instrument passing in front of his left shoulder. The 'cello has a greater variety of tone color than the viola, and is more often used as a solo instrument. A player must have ability to read the bass, tenor, and treble clefs, for all three clefs are used in writing music for the 'cello. The bass clef is most used.

The Double Bass

The double bass, often called bass viol, string bass, or contra bass, has four strings, tuned in fourths—G-D-A-E, as follows:

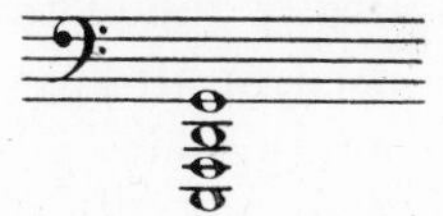

It will be noted from the illustration that the pitch of the double bass is quite low. In order to avoid using a great many leger lines when writing music for this instrument, the notes are written an octave higher than they sound. The tuning notation then would be as follows:

The chief function of the double bass is to furnish a bass foundation for the orchestra, often being assisted by the 'cellos, bassoons, trombones, or tuba. Early composers, such as Haydn and Mozart, used the double bass mostly for reinforcing the 'cellos of the orchestra, providing a deep, rich background of tone color. Later composers have gone further than this, however, and have written more independent parts for the instrument. Music for the double bass is generally in the bass clef, but occasionally the tenor clef appears. Sometimes even the treble clef must be employed, in order to show that "harmonics" * are to be played.

The Harp

The harp consists of a large, triangular frame of wood and metal, within which are stretched forty-six gut strings. The wide, hollow side of the instrument which rests against the player is a wooden soundboard, the purpose of which is to increase the tone resonance. The strings are tuned in half-steps and whole-steps to the scale of C-flat, but by pressing pedals at the base of the instrument, the

* On stringed instruments, high tones produced by bowing the string while lightly touched by a finger of the left hand.

harp may be automatically tuned to any key. The same fingering is therefore used in all keys.

The music written for the harp resembles piano music, but characteristic harp music for the orchestra consists mostly of arpeggio (broken chord) passages. However, simultaneous chords with each hand are possible.

WOOD-WIND INSTRUMENTS

The Flute and Piccolo

The flute is a slender tube having a system of keys for the fingers, by which the player can open and close holes in the instrument to produce different tones. In former years flutes were always made of wood, but nearly all flutes in use today are made of silver-plated metal.

All wind instruments are sounded by setting in vibration columns of air. A flute player causes the column of air within the flute to vibrate by directing a flow of breath across a hole near the end of the tube. The flute has a wonderfully pleasing tone of crystal clearness, its high and low register having such a variety of tone quality that it is useful for solo passages as well as for the ensemble.

The piccolo is simply a small flute, which produces tones an octave higher than those of the flute. The tones of the piccolo are shrill and piercing, and it ordinarily is used only when the full orchestra is playing forte or fortissimo.

The orchestra piccolo is built in the pitch of C, the same as the flute. The D-flat piccolo is generally used in bands.* Music for the piccolo is written one octave lower than it sounds. In a symphony orchestra, the third flute player generally doubles on the piccolo when it is needed.

The Oboe

The oboe, English horn, bassoon, and contra bassoon are made to produce tones by means of a double reed,

* Adoption of C piccolo is now being recommended.

which consists of two thin strips of cane placed together, with a small passage between them for air.

The clarinet, bass clarinet, and saxophone have single reeds, made from strips of cane. The reed is placed over an oblong-shaped opening in the mouthpiece, and rests against the player's lower lip.

The oboe, soprano member of the double-reed family of instruments, is a slender wooden instrument, with finger holes and keys. It has a penetrating, nasal quality of tone, suggesting oriental atmosphere or pastoral scenes. The players in a symphony orchestra usually tune their instruments to the "A" sounded by the oboe.

The English Horn

The English horn is really a tenor oboe tuned to the pitch of F, a fifth below that of the oboe. It is called a transposing instrument, because music for it must be written a fifth higher than it is to sound. The tone quality of the English horn is dark and melancholy, and this instrument is often used in solo passages to express sadness or mystery.

The Bassoon

The bassoon is considerably larger than the English horn, its wooden tubing being so long that it must be doubled upon itself for convenience in holding and playing. It is held in an almost vertical position; a curved mouthpiece, which holds the reed, projects from the instrument. The bassoon has a rather wide range of tones, and is useful in the orchestra in many ways. It is often employed in solo passages, and its peculiar tone is capable of expressing the idea of grotesqueness or humor. It is frequently used to reinforce the bass part, or to play in the middle part of the harmony. The bassoon is built in the pitch of C.

The Contra Bassoon

The contra bassoon has a greater length of tubing than the bassoon, and is pitched one octave lower. Music for it is written one octave higher than it sounds. It is used only occasionally in the orchestra for special effects.

The Clarinet

The clarinet has somewhat the same appearance as the oboe at a distance, but it is larger than the oboe and has a different system of fingering. The B-flat clarinet and the A clarinet are used the most in the orchestra, but occasionally the E-flat and the C clarinet are called for. The fingering for all these clarinets is the same, the difference being in size and pitch only. All except the C clarinet are transposing instruments, because music for them must be written in different keys from that which actually sounds. The tone quality of the clarinet is exceptionally clear and beautiful, and it is therefore often used for solo passages. Frequently it takes alto parts when the flute plays the melody, since the tones of the two blend remarkably well.

The Bass Clarinet

The bass clarinet is pitched in B-flat, one octave lower than the ordinary B-flat clarinet. Its shape resembles that of the saxophone, as it has a turned-up bell at the lower end and a curved crook at the mouthpiece end—both made of metal. The main part of the tubing is made of wood or metal. The tubing of the saxophone is made entirely of metal. The bass clarinet is used for playing solo passages, when a certain effect is desired, or may be used to play some lower part in the harmony.

BRASS-WIND INSTRUMENTS

The player of a brass-wind instrument not only blows air into the horn, but causes his lips to vibrate in a certain manner upon the cupped mouthpiece; by this means the column of air within the instrument is set in vibration. A considerable amount of practice and training is required to develop the muscles of the mouth properly, and to attain skill in correct breathing. The technique of mouth and lip adjustment in relation to the playing of both brass-wind and wood-wind instruments is called "embouchure" (pronounced ahm-bu-shur′), from the French word "bouche," meaning *mouth*.

A natural, or "harmonic," series of tones may be produced upon a brass-wind instrument by simply changing the position of the lips and using the proper amount of breath for each tone. Each tone of the scale has its own series of harmonics. Scale tones differing from those in the harmonic series of the tonic (5th, octave, 10th, 12th) are produced by means of "valves," manipulated with the fingers; in the case of the slide trombone, the player produces those tones by changing the position of the slide.

The flaring opening at the end of a wind instrument is called the "bell."

The French Horn

The French horn, generally referred to as the "horn," has sixteen feet of brass tubing, curled in a circular form. The modern horn is built in the pitch of F, but the type in use during the eighteenth and part of the nineteenth century was pitched in C, and was not provided with valves. Thus the composers of that period were limited to the use of the natural tone series when writing for the horn. The pitch of the horn could be changed, however, by inserting in the instrument bent pieces of tubing of various lengths, called "crooks." In effect, these crooks made the horn longer or shorter, and hence changed the pitch. If the key of a composition called for the B-flat series of natural tones, the B-flat crook was used; if the composition called for "Horn in E-flat," the E-flat crook, etc. The horn parts in orchestral music are to this day usually written without use of signature, just as music was written for the early "natural" horns, the sharps and flats being inserted throughout the part as accidentals. The modern horn is pitched in F (a perfect fifth below C). Music notation is written for it a perfect fifth higher than it will sound. The horn is therefore a transposing instrument.

Four horns are regularly employed in a symphony orchestra, although some compositions call for more or less than that number. The horn sounds to best advantage when used for sustained tones, but it is useful in many ways. It is very effective as a solo instrument and often is employed to double solos with other instruments.

The Trumpet and Cornet

The trumpet is composed of about eight feet of tubing, coiled about so that the length of the instrument is approximately eighteen inches. It is a transposing instrument, pitched in B-flat. The early type of trumpet, like the horn, had no valves and therefore required the use of crooks to change the pitch when necessary. With the addition of valves, the trumpet is able to play complete scales in any key, but if key signatures containing six and seven sharps or flats are encountered, the fingering becomes awkward and the player's technique is hampered in rapid passages. To avoid this the trumpet is equipped with a built-in crook which, when pulled out to a certain point, changes the pitch of the instrument from B-flat to A—one half tone lower. The advantage of this will be readily seen by taking for an example a composition written in the key of E (four sharps). If the composer writes for the B-flat trumpet, the signature for that instrument would be six sharps (key of F-sharp), because the notation for a B-flat instrument must be written one whole tone higher than it will sound. Now music written in such a key would involve complicated fingering, but if the trumpet part were written for "Trumpet in A," the signature would be one sharp (key of G), because the notes would then be written one and a half tones higher than they sound. The fingering problem would naturally be greatly simplified.

The use of the A crook has its disadvantage, however, in that the instrument will not play as accurately in tune as when it is left in the pitch of B-flat. Expert trumpet players have therefore accustomed themselves to playing the B-flat trumpet in all keys, preferring to master the fingering difficulties rather than tolerate the imperfect intonation of the A trumpet. When music is written for "Trumpet in A," such a player transposes his part, reading the notes as though they were written one half tone lower.

The regular staff of trumpet players in a symphony orchestra usually numbers three. The trumpets are especially valuable for reinforcing the other instruments in fortissimo passages; also for expressing military triumph, or jubilant, festive moods.

The cornet is also a B-flat instrument, and closely resembles the trumpet in appearance. The cornet is somewhat shorter and the tubing is usually of a larger bore. In tone, the cornet is full, rich, and mellow; the trumpet, brilliant and penetrating. A band may have two cornets to each trumpet; the cornets playing the solo and first parts, the trumpets the second and third parts.

The Trombone

The slide trombone is an important member of the brass-wind family, for it is not only capable of extreme power of tone in fortissimos, but it has a rich, resonant quality which is very effective in the more subdued passages. Various sizes of trombones are made, but the most commonly used is the B-flat tenor. The bass trombone is used occasionally. A long crook, called the "slide," fits into the instrument telescope fashion, and is moved in and out by the player to produce the various tones. The player uses seven different positions of the slide to produce tones, and in each position he is able to play a harmonic series of tones by means of lip adjustment. When the slide is completely in, it is in the first position. B-flat (second line, bass clef), and the harmonic series of tones above it are played in this position. When the slide is pushed outward to the second position, the tone A is produced; and so on, each succeeding position lowering the pitch by a semitone. The tone E (first leger line below the bass staff) is found in the seventh position, the slide fully extended.

Trombones are also made with valves instead of a slide, but their tone is not as flexible. Their only advantage is the ease of execution, since valves can be manipulated more rapidly than a slide.

Three slide trombones are ordinarily used in symphony orchestras; the bass trombone player usually doubles on a tenor trombone when needed. The trombone is not a transposing instrument; music for it is written just as it will sound, ordinarily in the bass clef.

The Tuba

The tuba, or "bass horn," is the largest of the brass-wind family, and therefore capable of the deepest tones. It is made in various shapes and sizes, and has three or four valves. One or two tubas, usually in the pitch of C, are used in symphony orchestras. The double B-flat tuba is larger, and is always used in bands. The E-flat tuba is a smaller instrument, also used in bands. Music is written for the tuba as it will sound, as in the case of all brass instruments reading the bass clef.

The tone of the tuba blends very well with that of the trombone, and it is often used with three trombones to form a brass quartet. Such a combination sounds to advantage when extreme fortissimos are desired from the entire orchestra.

The following instruments are used in the band, but are not regularly employed in symphony orchestras. The first four, the alto horn, the mellophone, the baritone and euphonium belong to the brass-wind family. The saxophone is related to the wood-wind instruments, but really belongs in a separate classification.

The Alto Horn

The alto horn is an "upright" instrument (bell pointing upward), built in the pitch of E-flat. Music for it is written a major sixth higher than it will sound. Alto horns are often used in bands when French horns are missing, in order to complete the full harmony. Parts are written for 1st, 2nd, 3rd, and 4th alto horns.

The Mellophone

Like the alto horn, the mellophone serves as a substitute for the French horn. It is a circular-shaped horn built in the pitch of F, and the player may read French horn parts without transposition. It is easy to learn to play, but its tone quality is inferior to that of the French horn. The mellophone is often employed in bands and in school orchestras when French horns are not available.

The Baritone Horn; Euphonium

The baritone horn is the "cello of the band." It is shaped like the upright alto horn, but is larger and is built in the pitch of B-flat. Music for the baritone is usually written in the bass clef, but is sometimes written in the treble clef. Bass clef parts are written as they will sound, but treble clef parts are written one tone higher than they will sound. The player uses a different system of fingering when reading the treble clef. Baritones are frequently used in school orchestras as substitutes for other instruments. In the band, they are usually assigned to counter-melodies or solo passages.

The Alto Clarinet

The alto clarinet is pitched in E♭, a fifth lower than the B-flat clarinet. It is similar to the bass clarinet in appearance, though smaller. Its solo timbre is distinctive and very necessary to the instrumentation of the concert band.

The Saxophone

The saxophone is made of conical brass tubing, having a turned-up bell and a curved neck. It is built in several sizes ranging from the soprano saxophone to the bass saxophone. It has a system of keys and pads somewhat like that of the clarinet, the sound being produced by means of a single reed. Saxophones are not regularly employed in symphony orchestras, but are pleasing in bands, especially when a complete "section" of saxophones is present. They are often used in school orchestras as substitutes for missing instruments. A section of three or more saxophones will usually be found in modern dance orchestras. The sizes most commonly used in bands and orchestras are the E-flat alto, the B-flat tenor, and the E-flat baritone, all of which are transposing instruments.

PERCUSSION INSTRUMENTS

The kettledrums or tympani, four of which are generally used in symphony orchestras, are the most important part of the percussion section. They resemble large copper bowls, and across the tops are stretched membranes, called "heads." Kettledrums, unlike other drums, can be tuned so that actual tones may be played upon them. Each kettledrum in the orchestra is of a different size, making available a large range of tones. The music frequently requires that the pitches of the kettledrums be changed several times during the playing of the composition, and it then becomes necessary for the player to place his ear close to the instrument and tune it while the orchestra is playing. The old fashioned type of kettledrum was tuned by means of screws which, when turned, tightened or loosened the head. The new type can be tuned much more rapidly, since the player needs only to press or release a pedal with his foot.

The kettledrums play a somewhat dramatic role in the orchestra. In fortissimo passages they intensify the excitement or accent the rhythm; in pianissimo they may be used to produce an effect of mystery.

The bass drum is usually used to accent the rhythm of fortissimos, but it can also be used very effectively in the more delicate passages.

The side drum (or snare drum) is a small drum upon which can be played a variety of rhythmic figures by means of two drum sticks. Across the under head are stretched several gut strings, called "snares;" hence the name "snare drum." The snares, when set in vibration by beats upon the drum, serve to increase the resonance and to make the drum sensitive to the slightest touch of the drum sticks.

Other percussion instruments include the cymbals, large discs of brass played by striking together; the triangle, a small steel bar bent in the shape of a triangle and played by striking with a short steel rod; the tambourine, a small drum with a single membrane head, played by striking with the hand; the castanets, small pairs of clappers held in the hands and clicked together; the gong, a suspended metal plate, sounded by striking with a bass drum stick;

the glockenspiel (bells), a set of metal bars played by striking with small metal hammers.

THE VOICE

So far, in the present chapter, we have been considering mechanical instruments only. Now we shall consider the natural instrument, one which is possessed and capable of being used by every normal person, the voice. As a musical instrument the voice is probably older than the mechanical instruments. We have no proof of this, but surmise leads us to this conclusion. Singing probably originated in the chanting of the hunters around the evening camp fire as they returned home from the chase. Each successful hunter would naturally desire to tell about his prowess. As time went on, in order to vary the description he probably let his voice rise and fall dramatically. Gradually, as rhythm came to be understood, this chant took on the form of a ballad, or a simple song telling a story. Another theory is that the priests, in religious incantations developed the rhythmic variations in pitch which we call singing.

Whether or not these theories are true, vocal music has steadily developed through the ages until it has become an integral part of our lives. Singing has been a part of the services of the church since time immemorial. Beginning with the chanting of the priests, this art has grown until today almost every church has its choir. The development of harmony was probably the most significant factor in the history of singing. As has already been pointed out, until about the fourteenth century, people were accustomed to sing in unison or in what might be called primitive harmony. By this we mean singing in octaves, fourths, or fifths, which to us is not harmony at all.

Difference Between Song and Speech

The method of breathing and of producing voice resonance are very much the same in both song and speech, but there are certain fundamental differences in other respects with which the student should be familiar.

First, a singer uses several series of tones and semitones, called scales, arranged in a definite order. He is required to sing each syllable of the words of a song in a certain pitch, determined by the music. In speech, however, he lets his voice rise and fall in a natural, individual manner, not confining his words to any definite tone-series.

Second, the singer sustains his vowels, and cuts short his consonants; in speech, the words are emitted in quicker succession, and vowels have about the same length as consonants.

Voices, like all other instruments, tend to be grouped into choirs. It is indeed fortunate that all of us do not possess the same type of voice. If we did, our choral singing would be most monotonous and uninteresting. The extreme range from the highest female voice to the lowest male voice, allows the composer to write a wide variety of musical patterns.

The highest voice is known as the *soprano*. It is almost impossible to describe the range of this voice because all sopranos differ. Music for sopranos, however, is not usually written above A above the treble staff, and seldom below middle C. *Coloratura* and *lyric* sopranos, however, are sometimes called upon to sing as high as C, two octaves above middle C. The word *coloratura,* as applied to sopranos, means a voice which is capable of singing the high, colorful, and florid passages used in opera and in concert. Oftentimes the coloratura passages are answered by the flute in the orchestra. The term *lyric* is also used in connection with sopranos as well as with tenors. It originally meant *song-like,* but has somehow lost its original meaning and now indicates the kind of song as well as the type of voice. When we say that a soprano has a lyric voice, we mean that the voice is smooth, high, and capable of passing from one pitch to another with agility. The term *dramatic soprano* means that the voice is capable of singing dramatic songs. This necessitates a powerful, full, rich, and resonant voice.

The alto voice is the low female voice. Music for it is seldom written above treble fourth space E, and seldom below G below middle C. The solo voice of the alto section is known as *contralto* (contra-alto) and is usually lower than the alto voice. In addition to being lower than the soprano voice, the alto usually has a deeper, richer, and more "reedy" quality.

The *tenor* voice is the high male voice. Music is seldom written for this voice higher than treble second line G, and seldom lower than bass second space C. Two general classifications of the tenor voice are used. We speak of *tenor-robusto* (robust tenor) to mean a voice with vitality, capable of singing operatic, or dramatic songs. A *lyric* tenor is one who can sing, like the lyric soprano, high passages with a smooth quality and style.

The *baritone* is the solo voice of the low male voices. Music for it is sometimes written as high as treble second line G, and as low as bass first line G. The operatic baritone must be prepared to sing in a greater range than any of the other voices except the soprano.

The *bass* is the lowest masculine voice, and is sometimes asked to sing as low as the first added line below the bass staff. This voice is usually quite powerful, and there are many more of them than tenors. To compensate for having to sing so low, the bass seldom has to sing above middle C.

When voices are used in combination, names are assigned to the group according to the number of voices in the group. The table below shows these names as they are assigned to the voice groups:

NO. OF VOICES	GROUP NAME
one	solo
two	duet or duo
three	trio
four	quartet
five	quintet
six	sextet
seven	septet
eight	octet
nine	choir

The most common and most well known group is the quartet. When mixed voices are used, they are soprano, alto, tenor, and bass. When male voices only are used, they are first tenor, second tenor, first bass (or baritone), and second bass. A quartet of female voices consists of two sopranos and two altos.

During the course of musical history, a multitude of beautiful music has been written for these voice groups. As has been pointed out, the greatest amount has been written for quartets. This, of course, includes all the music that has been written for choruses and choirs since it is customarily written in four parts and can be sung by either a quartet or a choir. This is true both in the sacred and secular fields, and it is possible to hear both types at almost any time. Various radio stations have their staff choruses, and they keep in their libraries thousands of choral numbers illustrative of all the historical periods.

Two types of choral singing are in vogue at present, as they have been for several hundred years. *A cappella* (unaccompanied) choirs originated in the Catholic church, but have grown until they are common to church, community and school. The type of music sung by these choirs differs somewhat from that of accompanied choirs. Since there is no accompaniment, the scope of the music is much more narrow. Usually it is smooth and flowing because it is limited in kind of tone that may be used. An accompaniment may be used but as it would merely duplicate the voice parts, the singing is much more beautiful without it. Polyphonic music is used a great deal with a cappella choirs. The other type of choir is the accompanied choir. There is much more music written for choir with accompaniment, although the a cappella choir was in existence before the accompanied choir. Most churches and schools use the accompanied choir, as the music is usually more simple and singing is easier when following a piano or an organ.

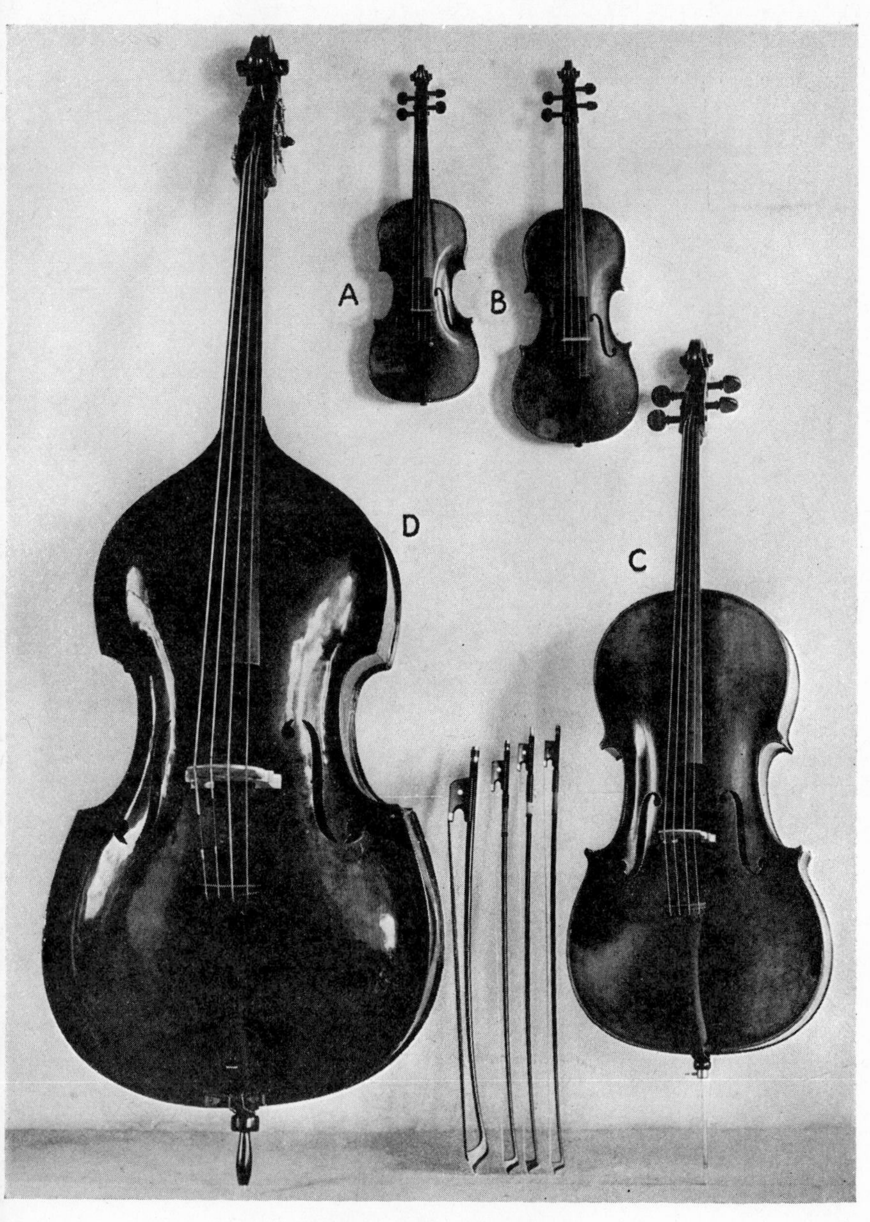

STRING INSTRUMENTS

A Violin
B Viola
C Violoncello *('cello)*
D Double Bass

Bows (Left to Right): Double Bass, 'Cello, Viola, Violin

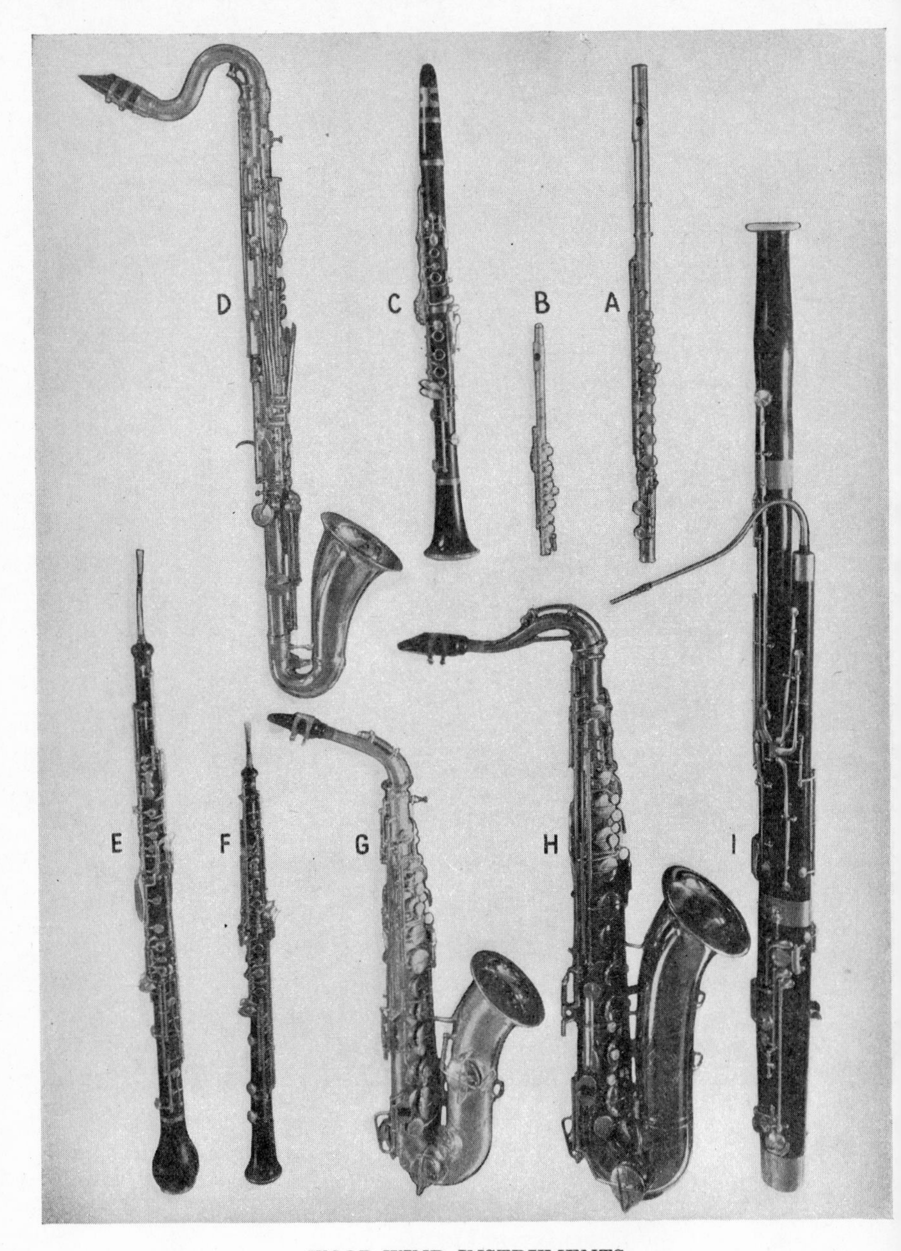

WOOD-WIND INSTRUMENTS

A Flute
B Piccolo
C B♭ Clarinet
D B♭ Bass Clarinet
E English Horn
F Oboe
G E♭ Alto Saxophone
H B♭ Tenor Saxophone
I Bassoon

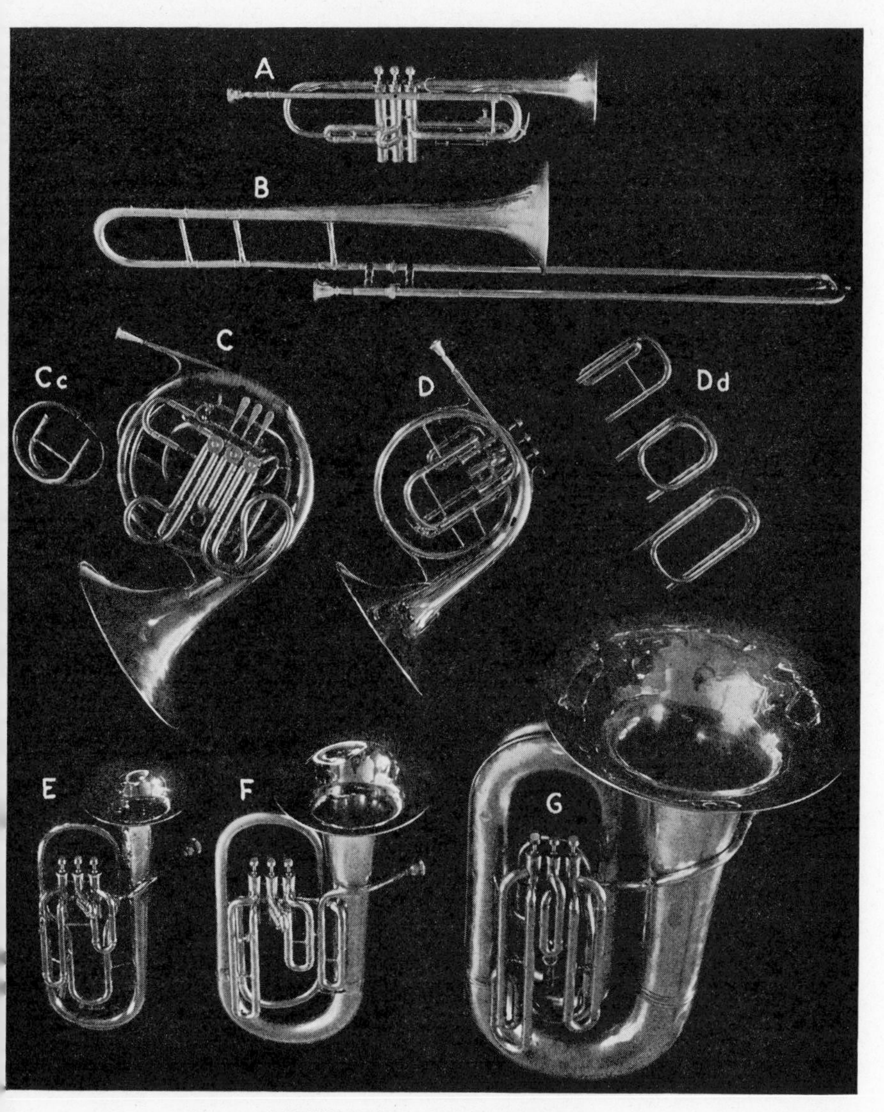

BRASS-WIND INSTRUMENTS

A Trumpet
B Trombone
C French Horn
Cc Crook for French Horn
D Mellophone
Dd Crooks for Mellophone
E E♭ Alto Horn
F Baritone
G Tuba

PERCUSSION INSTRUMENTS

A Snare Drum
B Cymbals
C Tambourine
D Kettledrum *(with tuning pedal)*
E Bass Drum

CHAPTER VI

BRIEF BIOGRAPHIES OF GREAT COMPOSERS

"I am a part of all I have met."—RALPH WALDO EMERSON

THE HISTORY of the world is really the history of men and women. History is made by *people,* not by dates and events. It is sometimes said that the men who know most about history are the men who have made a study of the lives of great people. Dates in themselves are not at all important. They merely assist us in placing men and events in their proper order. It clarifies our picture to know that when some certain event was happening in one part of the world, similar events were occurring in others, and that certain great men in one country lived at the same time as the great men of another. It is interesting, for example, to know that the first piano brought into the United States, came during the administration of George Washington. It is the *time relationship* that is important.

Probably the most important part of the history of music, then, is related in the lives of the great composers. Writers of great music have lived and died, and left to us great masterpieces of music which will live immortal in the lives of music lovers and the world at large. Raphael, Michelangelo, and Corot left us great works of art to be seen and admired. But Bach, Beethoven, and Brahms left no works of art, but mere directions for *reproducing* them. An "original" painting deteriorates with time and can belong to but one person at a time. The art of the master musicians is timeless and belongs to whomever is able to interpret their printed directions.

It is in the lives of the great composers then that we find the real history of music. The inspiration to discover for ourselves the true meaning and wonder of great masterpieces of music can come only from a sympathetic study of the events in their lives. To know the famous music masters is to admire and love them, and to love *them* means loving their *music* also.

Johann Sebastian Bach (1685-1750), considered by many authorities as the world's greatest musician, was born in Eisenach, Germany. He studied violin with his father until the latter's death when Johann was ten years old. His brother then took over his musical training, teaching him the organ and harpsichord. He had a sweet soprano voice which gave him a place in the choir and after his voice changed he remained as church organist. Hard study brought him rapid advancement and a position as violinist at Weimar. So intensely interested in music was he that on one occasion he walked over two hundred miles to hear Buxtehude play the organ. The inspiration of this great organist started him composing and in this work his fame grew rapidly. He married Mana Bach, one of his cousins, and shortly thereafter was appointed musical director of St. Thomas school at Leipzig. He was interested for the most part in writing cantatas, fugues, and sonatas. Much of the development of the art of violin playing in this period was due to the many fine violin sonatas produced by Bach. Married twice, he was the father of twenty-one children, a number of whom became fine musicians. At the age of sixty-four Bach became totally blind, and died within a year. Many of his best works were published after his death.

Although Bach's works are too numerous to mention in detail (some authors estimate them at about 1500) some of the best known are "The Well Tempered Clavichord," consisting of forty-eight preludes and fugues in different keys, the "Passion of St. Matthew," the "Brandenburg Concertos," the "Christmas Oratorio," and the "B Minor Mass." He introduced the use of the thumb in clavier playing, was the foremost contrapuntal composer, and wrote in almost every musical form.

Georg Friedrich Handel (1685-1759) was born in Saxony, a German province. A child prodigy, he had already composed several sonnets at the age of ten. At eighteen, he went to Hamburg to play violin in the opera house. He was so efficient that he was soon made director, and the work inspired him to write his first opera, "Almira." Handel possessed a violent temper which was always causing trouble with his fellow musicians. After a serious duel with one of them he went to Italy. Here he was very successful in writing more operas. He was selected to manage a newly founded musical academy, but his temper again was the cause of much trouble. In another business venture he lost about $50,000, which nearly caused him to give up his musical career. He turned to writing oratorios, "Esther" being the first, and others following in rapid succession. He then went to England and Ireland where he wrote and produced his "Messiah," the best known and most popular of his works. The king of England engaged him to write music for a royal river party, and Handel wrote his "Water Music" for the occasion. He, like Bach, became totally blind at the last and died at the age of seventy-four. Although his operas are seldom produced, excerpts are heard frequently, and his contributions to the field of oratorio will long be remembered.

Franz Joseph Haydn (1732-1809) was born in Austria, of poor parents. As a small child he showed a remarkable talent for music, and at the age of eight was received into the choir of a church in Vienna. At twenty he had composed his first quartet for strings. Ten years later he was engaged as a musical director by Count Morzin, receiving a small salary and board and room. After two years, Prince Esterhazy placed him at the head of his private chapel where he composed most of his beautiful symphonies and string quartets. After the death of the prince, Haydn went to England where he produced six of his twelve symphonies. He was a great friend of the Prince of Wales who used to play the cello, accompanied by Haydn at the harpsichord. Shortly before his death he composed "The Creation" and "The Seasons." His great contributions to musical literature include his twelve symphonies, many string quartets and other chamber music, and his oratorios.

Wolfgang Amadeus Mozart (1756-1791) was born in Salzburg, Germany, a son of a fine violinist. At the age of four, he began studying with his father, and learned to play minuets and other small pieces on the harpsichord. At the age of five he composed a concerto for the harpsichord which was so difficult that only a finished performer could play it. When he was six, his father took him to Munich where they were received at court with great favor. At seven, he went to Paris where he played the most difficult music of Bach and Handel. At fourteen he had composed his first opera, which was performed more than twenty times. Returning to Salzburg, he was appointed court organist and composer, but found that he had to teach in order to make ends meet. In spite of his poverty, it was here that he wrote his best music, the "Marriage of Figaro," "Don Giovanni," the "Magic Flute," and others. He died at the early age of thirty-five and was buried in a pauper's grave.

Ludwig van Beethoven (1770-1827), one of the first composers of the romantic period, was born in Germany. His musical talent was noticed by his father, who began his training. His father, a drunkard, would reel home late at night and rouse young Ludwig out of bed to practice Bach and Handel for hours. This gave the lad an intense dislike for practice, but could not kill his love for the music. He began to compose and won the admiration of Mozart. He moved to Vienna, became an earnest student, and although very poor and uncouth, made many friends. At the age of forty he became deaf, but continued with his composing. Many of his best works were written after he could no longer hear them. His deafness caused him to be ill-tempered, irritable, and moody. He never married, and died in Vienna at the age of fifty-seven. He wrote in many styles: for the orchestra, piano, voice, and chamber music. His only known opera is "Fidelio." He wrote one oratorio, the "Mount of Olives." He wrote two hundred and fifty songs, thirty-two sonatas for the piano, nine for violin, nine symphonies, and many other compositions. His "Moonlight Sonata" is probably his most popularly known piano composition.

Carl Maria Von Weber (1786-1826) was born in Germany, the son of a theatrical and musical family. His early life was spent in touring Germany with his parents giving concerts, the family furnishing most of the performers. He studied under Michael Haydn, brother of the famous Franz Joseph. At the age of fourteen he composed an opera which he called the "Wood Maiden." His acquaintance and admiration for Haydn and Beethoven inspired him to take up the study of music seriously. While still a young man he became conductor of a theater orchestra in Breslau but left to take up the duties of secretary to the Duke of Wurtem. After leaving this position he composed his most famous opera, "Der Freischutz." "Euryanthe" and "Oberon" soon followed. His work and theatrical compositions took him to many places in Europe but the strenuous travel and hard work caused him to contract tuberculosis. He died of this disease in 1826. His best known piano composition was the "Invitation to the Dance," the first piece of dance music to be used on the concert platform.

Giacomo Meyerbeer (1791-1864), whose real name was Jacob Beer, was the son of wealthy Jewish parents in Berlin, Germany. His musical talent as a lad was so marked that his parents procured the services of Clementi as a piano teacher. At the age of seven he had played Mozart's D minor Concerto in public. Becoming an accomplished virtuoso, he turned to composition, producing several operas. Failing in Germany, however, he went to Italy where he was more successful. From Italy he went to Paris and settled down to a study of French customs and traditions, writing them successfully into several well known and popular operas. Among them were "Les Huguenots," "Le Prophete," and "L' Africaine," the latter being performed for the first time two years after his death. Meyerbeer achieved importance in the field of composition because of his ability to write in many styles and moods, and because of his work in increasing facility in orchestral technique.

Gioachino Antonio Rossini (1792-1868) was born in Pesaro, Italy. As a boy of ten he added to the family income by playing cello, horn, and piano. He early felt the spell of operas, and it is in this field that he excelled and did most of his work. He was an admirer of Mozart, whose works he imitated. He soon became known for his fine melodies, and his ability to write for the orchestra. This ability is probably best known through his "William Tell." He wrote in various styles and his sacred choral works "Stabat Mater," and "Solemn Mass" show this versatility. His best known opera is probably the "Barber of Seville" which is known as "opera buffa," or comic opera.

Franz Peter Schubert (1797-1828), was born in Vienna, Austria, of poor but musical parents. His father and older brothers gave him his early training in music. When Franz was eleven, he was accepted in the church choir, where he remained until the age of sixteen, studying music under the choirmaster. He soon began conducting the school orchestra and taught elementary subjects in his father's school. While here he composed one of his best known compositions, "The Erlking." He was very fond of the music of Mozart and Beethoven, and the inspiration of their works led him into various forms of composition. He wrote about five hundred songs, ten symphonies, and several masses. His unbusinesslike methods led him into miserable poverty and a mean existence. His best known songs are probably "Hark, Hark, the Lark," and "Ave Maria," and his best known symphony, the "Unfinished Symphony." He died two years after Beethoven and at his own request was buried beside him. He will be remembered as one of the world's greatest melodists.

Hector Berlioz (1803-1869) was born in France. His father, a physician, sent him to Paris to study medicine, but the flute and guitar were more interesting to him. He began studying music, singing in a theater to pay for his lessons. He tried writing a cantata and after many failures, finally won the "Prix de Rome." This entitled him to three years musical study at home and abroad. He possessed a restless nature, and returned in less than two years. After attempting more compositions without great success, he became the leading critic for the city newspaper. He continued to compose, however, and at last his works began to receive attention. He became outstanding as a conductor by finding new ways to combine the orchestral instruments to produce new effects. And it is in this field that he is so significant to music. He introduced voices into his symphonies and called them "dramatic symphonies." Among the best known and most popular are "Romeo and Juliet," "Harold in Italy," and the "Damnation of Faust."

Felix Mendelssohn-Bartholdy * (1809-1847) was born in Hamburg, Germany, of a wealthy and intellectual family. He was one of four children, and he and his sister Fanny

* See Chapter VII.

took an early interest in music. A real friendship developed between the two which continued throughout their lives. Mendelssohn's first musical instruction began in Berlin, where at the age of ten he was playing in public, and at twelve was composing for piano and voice. He received a great deal of benefit from the many visits of literary and musical people at his home which was a gathering place for famous people. He began composing a great deal of music and through it became so popular that some of the older musicians became jealous of him, causing him much unhappiness. He accepted a position as conductor at Leipzig where he did a great deal of composing, one of his compositions being the famous oratorio "St. Paul." Here also he met a Swiss clergyman's daughter whom he married. He founded a music conservatory at Leipzig and his time became entirely taken up with his activities. He continued composing, however, but overwork and the death of his sister Fanny caused his own death. His best known piano composition is probably the "Spring Song." Two other oratorios have become well known, "Elijah," and the "Hymn of Praise." His overture to "Midsummer Night's Dream" is one of the best examples of well written music we have. He was a great admirer of both Bach and Handel and their influence is seen in most of his work in the oratorio field.

Frederic Francois Chopin (1810-1849) was born near Warsaw, Poland. His father was a teacher in the University, and his mother a Polish noblewoman. At the age of nine his musical talent was noted when he played a difficult piano concerto with great success. By the age of thirteen he had composed several difficult piano pieces. At eighteen he went to Vienna where he was recognized as one of the greatest piano virtuosi of his day. While in Vienna he wrote three nocturnes for the piano, a number of etudes, or studies, and a concerto which he dedicated to Liszt. His health was never the best, and hard work in composition made him the victim of consumption at the age of thirty. He went to southern France for his health and here met George Sand, with whom he fell desperately in love. Her inspiration was responsible for much of his delightful music. He was known in his day as one of the greatest of pianists, and he is remembered as one of the greatest of the composers of piano music. His waltzes, preludes and etudes are models of perfection used by a large proportion of students of the piano.

Robert Schumann (1810-1856) was born in Germany at Zwickau. Although his parents were not particularly musical, young Robert acquired a great desire to practice and study. At the age of twelve he was quite an accomplished pianist. His mother set her heart on making him a lawyer, but he cared very little for his law studies. His mind being on music most of the time, it was only natural that he should become an excellent performer even while studying law. So anxious was he to become a really great pianist that he used a device for stretching his hand, and in doing so strained it to such an extent that he was unable to use it. He then turned to composing. He also wrote articles for and edited a musical journal for a number of years. He fell in love with his old teacher's daughter, Clara Wieck. His parents, however, opposed their marriage and an elopement followed. Many hardships beset the young couple, but the wife, also a musician, was of great help. Schumann became a teacher in the Leipzig conservatory, but was not a successful teacher. Overwork finally brought on insanity and attempted suicide. After three years in an asylum, death came. Schumann wrote about two hundred fifty songs for voice, many piano compositions, among which his works for children are very popular, several operas and cantatas, and five symphonies. His "Traumerei" is known all over the world.

Franz Liszt (1811-1886) was born in Hungary, the son of an official of Prince Esterhazy's court. His father, a fine pianist, gave him his first lessons. When he was nine years old, he showed such promise that his father was guaranteed enough to finance his education for six years. He was sent to Vienna where he met Schubert and once played for Beethoven. Paganini's violin playing so inspired him that he resolved to become as great a pianist as Paganini was a violinist. He succeeded so well that he became the idol of all Europe. Liszt lived for a time with gypsies in order to study their music and customs. He is famous for his gypsy music, his rhapsodies, fantasies, and classic orchestral works. "Liebestraum" is probably his best known piano composition, and has been popularized recently on the radio and in dance form.

Richard Wagner (1813-1883), probably the greatest of the opera composers, was born in Leipzig, Germany, where he received most of his education. He was interested in literature, Greek, and music. He was a hard worker and spent most of his spare time composing. At the age of twenty-two, he took his new opera the "Flying Dutchman" to Paris for production, but it was not well received. He struggled with financial difficulties for a number of years, always writing music, however. Exiled from Germany because of his political views, he was received with favor by the Bavarian king, who made it possible for him to devote his entire time to composition. During this period he wrote many of his best operas. Wagner's contributions to music were a large number of masterful operas, and the responsibility for introducing a new conception of opera. He believed that a perfect musical drama was a union of the three arts, poetry, music, and drama. His best known operas are "Die Meistersinger," "Parsifal," the "Nibelungen Ring," "Lohengrin," "Tannhauser," and "Tristan and Isolde."

Giuseppe Verdi (1813-1901) was born in Italy in the same year as Richard Wagner. At the age of ten he was made organist in the village church. After studying in Milan, he wrote and produced his first opera, "Oberto." Later he tried to write comic opera but with little success. He then went to London to study English opera, and returning to Italy devoted his time to writing "Rigoletto," "Il Trovatore," "Aida," and "Falstaff," all of which were successful. In addition to being a musician, Verdi was a member of the Italian parliament and later a senator. He was decorated for his musical achievements by the rulers of Russia and Egypt. He died in Milan after a long and successful career at the age of eighty-eight.

Charles Francois Gounod (1818-1893) was born in Paris, France, and received his education at the Paris conservatory. At twenty-one he received the Prix de Rome in composition. He then went to Rome to study the works of Palestrina and Bach. He became so discouraged by the failure of his music that he contemplated becoming a monk. However, his "St. Cecelia Mass" attracted attention and he found himself on the road to popularity. His first opera "Sappho" was unsuccessful, but he continued writing and soon produced "Faust," which became known as his most famous opera. It has since been performed at the Paris Opera over one thousand times. In addition to "Faust" and "Romeo and Juliet," the oratorio "The Redemption" is probably his best known work. A short cantata, "Gallia," is especially well known in this country.

Cesar Franck (1822-1890) was born in Liege, Belgium. At the age of fifteen he began his studies at the Paris Conservatory and received the first prize at graduation. He spent the remainder of his life in Paris, teaching, composing, and playing the organ. His major contribution to the field of music was in breaking away from the French style of composition. He was an idealist and intensely religious.

His best known work is probably the "Beatitudes" in oratorio form. His orchestral works include a great symphony in D minor, several symphonic poems, and symphonic variations. He also wrote much chamber music, some piano and organ music, and a number of songs.

Anton Rubinstein (1830-1894) was born in Russia, and early displayed remarkable musical talent. At the age of ten he was taken to Paris by his piano teacher, and there he played for Liszt and Chopin. After studying composition in Berlin, he journeyed through several European countries on a concert tour and was received everywhere with enthusiasm. By the time he was twenty-three he had composed two operas. After another tour, he was appointed organist in St. Petersburg, where he founded the Imperial Conservatory. For the next twenty-five years he made a number of world tours as a pianist and conductor, and did a great deal of composing. He once refused an offer of $125,000 for a tour of the United States. His compositions included thirteen operas, six symphonies, the best known of which is the "Ocean Symphony," and many piano compositions. Probably he is known the world over for his "Melody in F."

Johannes Brahms (1833-1897) was born in Hamburg, Germany. His father was a musician and helped with Johannes' early education. While still a boy, young Brahms displayed a great deal of ability and at the age of fourteen played a piano concert. When he was twenty he made a tour of Europe with the famous violinist Remenyi. During this period he met Liszt and Schumann, both of whom predicted a brilliant future for him. He finally settled in Vienna where he led a quiet life, conducting occasionally and composing continually. He was a thorough detailist, and always worked out his music in the classic manner, yet adding new touches of color and novel and complex effects. His principal works are piano pieces, a concerto for violin, four symphonies, and the "German Requiem." Students remember him best for his "Lullaby," or "Cradle Song," as it is sometimes called.

Charles Camille Saint-Saens (1835-1921) was born in Paris, and began the study of the piano at the age of three. He gave a concert at ten, and wrote his first symphony at sixteen. He studied at the Paris Conservatory under Gounod, and remained in Paris as an organist, teacher, and composer. He had a profound knowledge of the theory of music, and wrote in many and varied styles. In addition to five symphonies, he wrote four symphonic poems, and two orchestral suites. The opera "Samson and Delilah," and "Danse Macabre" for orchestra are probably his best known compositions.

Peter Ilyitch Tschaikowsky (1840-1893) was born in a mining region in the Ural district in Russia. At the age of eight he began the study of the piano. His father became the director of the school of Technology in St. Petersburg, and Peter began the study of law in the same institution. He continued the study of the piano, however, and after some work with Rubinstein, was appointed professor of harmony at the St. Petersburg Conservatory. His first works as a composer were unsuccessful but he continued to write and finally won recognition. He is noted mainly for his six symphonies, of which the "Pathetique" is probably the best known. He also wrote some chamber music, including the "Andante Cantabile," a movement from one of his string quartets, and a number of vocal compositions.

Antonin Dvorak (1841-1904) was born in Bohemia. His father was a butcher and wanted young Antonin to follow in his footsteps, but the boy's love for music soon caused him to leave home. As a child he used the violin belonging to the schoolmaster for practice, and studied piano and organ at the same time. When he was sixteen he went to Prague to study organ, and here he fell into financial difficulties. He was helped by Smetana, a musician and composer, who made it possible for him to study seriously, and to write music. His first fame came through the publication of his "Slavonic Dances." He left a position as professor of music at the Prague Conservatory to become a director of a conservatory in New York at a salary of $15,000 per year. After a few years, however, he left America to return home. He wrote a great deal of music, including five symphonies, several symphonic poems, many pieces of chamber music, an oratorio, and many songs. Dvorak is perhaps best known for his "New World Symphony" and "Humoreske."

Sir Arthur Sullivan (1842-1900) was born in England and received his early musical education as a choir boy in the Chapel Royal. He studied at the Royal Academy also, and then went to Leipzig to enter the conservatory there. While attending the conservatory he wrote the music of Shakespeare's "Tempest," and became famous overnight. He returned to England as professor of music at the Royal Academy, and also busied himself with organ playing, conducting and composing. He wrote many anthems and cantatas, orchestral music, and an oratorio. "The Prodigal Son" and the "Golden Legend," two of his cantatas, are very well known in this country. His chief contribution to music was in the field of light opera. In collaboration with W. S. Gilbert, a lyricist, he wrote and produced many famous light operas. Among the better known are "The Mikado," "The Pirates of Penzance," "Iolanthe," "H. M. S. Pinafore," and the "Gondoliers."

Edvard Hagerup Grieg (1843-1907) was born in Bergen, Norway. Receiving his first lessons from his mother, he was noticed by Ole Bull, a famous violinist, and through his insistence was sent to Leipzig for study. After four years at Leipzig, where he did some composing, he went to Copenhagen. Here he formed a friendship with

Nordraak, a Norwegian composer, and through him became interested in the folk music of his native land. He gave a series of concerts, taught, conducted, and composed a large number of songs and piano pieces. He possessed a rather retiring nature and returned to his home, spending his last years there in composition. He died at the age of sixty-four. His "Peer Gynt Suite" is often played.

Nikolai Rimsky-Korsakow (1844-1908) was born in the province of Novgorod, Russia. He early displayed unusual musical talent but was sent to the Naval Academy to study. After completing his course, he made a tour of the world as a midshipman. During this tour he composed his first symphony which was produced upon his return. He then devoted himself entirely to music. Many of his best works are taken from the Russian folk melodies. In addition to his symphonic and piano works, he wrote thirteen operas and overtures. His best known opera is probably "The Snow Maiden," and his best known orchestral suite "Scheherezade." When he was twenty-seven, he became a professor at the conservatory in St. Petersburg where he remained until his death.

Ignaz Jan Paderewski (1860) was born in Poland, and throughout his life has endeared himself to the Polish people by his intense loyalty and patriotism. Study at the conservatory in Warsaw decided him to take up a career as a piano virtuoso. He went to Vienna where he studied under Leschetizky and made several concert tours. He soon became established as one of the greatest piano virtuosi. His opera "Manru" contains many delightful melodies, as does his opera "Sakuntala." In addition to the operas, he has written numerous piano and violin pieces, and some songs. His "Ancient Minuet" or "Minuet in G" as it is sometimes called, is known the world over. Paderewski is famous as a diplomat and statesman as well as a composer, having served as Premier of Poland.

Edward Alexander MacDowell (1861-1908), the best known American composer, was born in New York City. He studied both at home and in Europe, and remained abroad to teach. In 1888, however, he returned to America to become professor of music at Columbia University. Later he resigned, due to ill health. He was promptly recognized as a great composer through the publication of his first piano suite. He has written symphonic poems, suites, concertos for the piano, sonatas, and numerous piano pieces. He was also well known as an educator, writing critical and historical essays. Among his best known compositions are the "Indian Suite," and two groups of small compositions published under the titles of "Woodland Sketches" and "Sea Pieces."

Claude Achille Debussy (1862-1918) was born in St. Germain, France. He received his musical training at the Paris Conservatory, and because of outstanding work in composition was awarded many prizes including the Prix de Rome, at the age of twenty-two. He rapidly rose to prominence in Paris, and throughout Europe by breaking away from the older traditions in composition. Debussy is an important figure in the field of composition because he heralded the new modern movement. He enjoyed writing in whole tones and using the primary overtones. He is sometimes known as the father of modern music, although he was not the first to write it. His best known works include the opera "Pelleas et Melisande," and the "Afternoon of a Faun" for orchestra.

Richard Strauss (1864), another composer of modern music, was born in Munich. His father was a horn player in the Munich Opera Company. Young Strauss early displayed musical talent, and began his study at the age of six. At sixteen some of his works were already being produced. He has spent most of his life conducting in Weimar, Vienna and Berlin, where he was director general of the Berlin Opera. As a conductor he has traveled as extensively as any other composer. His best known operas are "Salome," "Electra," and "Der Rosenkavalier," and for orchestra, "Ein Heldenleben," "Till Eulenspiegel's Merry Pranks," and "Don Juan." He has written several symphonies, several other symphonic poems, operas, and many fine songs.

Jean Sibelius (1865) was born in Tavastehus, Finland. His musical talent was discovered while he was yet a small boy, but he began the study of law at Helsingfors University. However, the call of music was strong upon him and he entered the conservatory, and then finished his studies in Berlin. In 1893 he returned to his native country and began to write music. After three years of writing and teaching, he had become so famous that the Finnish government offered him a life grant so that he might write exclusively. Sibelius is of a retiring disposition, yet one of the most strongly national of our present composers. He has written seven symphonies, several symphonic poems, and a great many smaller works. Probably the most popular of his compositions are his "Valse Triste," and the tone poem "Finlandia."

Sergei Rachmaninoff (1873), distinguished pianist and composer, was born in Onega, Russia. At nineteen he had already achieved fame as a pianist and conductor. After several concert tours, he accepted the position as conductor of the Moscow Opera, and then as conductor of the Moscow Symphony Orchestra. He visited the United States in 1909, and again in 1918, and then because of social problems in Russia, made this country his home. He has written several short operas, several symphonies and symphonic poems, many delightful piano pieces and a number of songs. All students are familiar with his "Prelude" in C-sharp minor.

Fritz Kreisler (1875), one of the world's most distinguished violinists, was born in Vienna, Austria. He began his studies with his father, then went to the Vienna and Paris conservatories. At only twelve years of age he had received the first prize at the conservatory. At fourteen he toured the United States giving violin concerts. For the next ten years he studied medicine and art, and finally went into military service, becoming an officer in the Uhlans. However, music had claimed him for its own, so he resumed his career, and soon became known as one of the finest violinists of all time. He has written a comic opera, a string quartet, and many very popular violin melodies. Among the latter, are included such favorites as the "Old Refrain," "Caprice Viennois," "Liebesfreud," and "Tamborin Chinois."

Maurice Ravel (1875) was born in Ciboure, France. At the age of twelve, his musical ability was so marked that he was taken to Paris for study, and at fourteen had entered the Paris Conservatory. His interest in the piano led him to study the works of Liszt, who, in addition to some of the Russian composers, of whom Ravel was very fond, influenced his music. He is known as an ultra-modern composer. His compositions are not as well known as those of older composers, but everyone is familiar with his "Bolero." He has written many piano pieces, some chamber music, considerable work for orchestra, and a number of songs.

Igor Stravinsky (1882) was born near St. Petersburg, Russia. His father was an operatic singer who discovered his son's remarkable musical talent. However, young Igor studied law until, at the age of twenty-two he met Rimsky-Korsakow who advised him to take up music as a profession. Stravinsky has become famous as a pianist and composer chiefly through his ultra-modern music. Like Debussy and Ravel, he was not satisfied with the old musical forms, and expresses himself in new ways, employing peculiar rhythms and chords. Most of his best known works have been written for orchestra, although he has also written a number of piano pieces, dramatic works, and songs. Probably among his more familiar music is his "Nightingale," an opera, and two ballets, the "Firebird," and "Petroushka."

[For selected references for Chapter VI see page 139]

CHAPTER VII

MUSICAL ANECDOTES

"The man that hath no music in himself,
Nor is not moved with concord of sweet sounds,
Is fit for treasons, stratagems, and spoils."

SHAKESPEARE

HERO WORSHIP is as old as man's history. It is only natural that we should look up to and revere the people who have accomplished great things. There are first of all, a great many names in history and in contemporary affairs that we all admire; names that stand for great deeds, great achievements, great thoughts recorded in books, and great military accomplishments. These names mean a lot to all of us. Then there are names that have a particular meaning for people in certain fields of activity. For example, the names of Pasteur, Harvey, and Lister are significant to people interested in medicine; the names of Galton, Thorndike, and Terman, are most familiar to people interested in Psychology; and the names of Marshall, Hughes, and Blackstone to those interested in law. Bach, Beethoven, and Brahms are merely names to the vast majority of people, but they become especially meaningful to the musician.

A common human tendency is to believe whatever appears in print. This is a sort of book worship and is called *bibliolatry*. It is obviously based on a faulty premise—that because it is printed it must be true. Hero worship is the same kind of tendency. It too rests on a shaky foundation because many of our heroes are just as capable of making mistakes as we are. However, it is a human failing, and is excusable in that many great people come nearer to being perfect than the rest of us. Famous musicians are worth studying because they were so expert in their art, and have made thrilling musical history by which we have all profited. That they were human too is revealed in the more intimate events of their daily lives. The present chapter is concerned with some of the interesting anecdotes about well known musicians that are not often encountered by the casual reader.

Arne, Thomas (1710–1778)

Thomas Arne, famous English composer, was like Handel in that he also used to steal away to the attic at night to practice on the harpsichord. So earnest in his practice was he, that he was an accomplished player at an early age. The story is told that on one occasion his father called upon a friend and was asked to go upstairs and listen to a concert. The elder Arne's surprise may be imagined when, on entering the room he found the concert being played by his own son.

Bach, Johann Sebastian (1685–1750)

The early life of Johann Sebastian Bach was not without its trials. His father and mother died when he was only nine years old and he went to live with his brother Johann Christoph. Christoph was a musician and taught Bach to play the clavier. Christoph also owned one of the few printed copies of a music book which young Bach particularly liked. He used to plead with his brother to let him play from it, but Christoph was unwilling to let so valuable a book out of his possession. One night the little boy stole out of bed, took the book out of the case, admired it and hummed its melodies for hours. Repeating this performance night after night, he began copying by moonlight the melodies in a book of his own. When he had the book almost completed, his brother discovered what he had been doing and destroyed the copy which had taken so many hours.

Bauer, Harold (1873)

Harold Bauer the famous pianist, and Claude Debussy, the late composer, were intimate friends. However, one subject was always a source of argument between them. Debussy contended that he wrote more difficult music than any other modern composer, and that no one could really play it properly. Bauer answered his argument by playing his most difficult compositions at sight. Finally Debussy thought he had won the dispute by writing a three tone chord, using the highest and the lowest notes on the piano keyboard, and one in the middle. However, Bauer played the chord by using one finger of each hand for the low and high notes, and for the middle one, his nose!

Brahms, Johannes (1833–1897)

On one occasion, when Brahms was playing a joint concert with a violinist friend, the piano they were asked to use was pitched one half tone lower than it should have been. Nothing daunted, Brahms played through the whole of Beethoven's Sonata one half tone higher than it was written so that the violin music would fit.

Brahms once paid a visit to his aging father, and while there, called his attention to a copy of Handel's "Saul." "Father," he said, "if things go badly with one, the best consolation is in music. Read carefully in my old 'Saul,' and you'll find what you need." After his departure, the old man looked within the copy and found bank notes between the pages!

Although Brahms never married and had no children of his own, he loved young folks and had them constantly around him. He was inspired by his little friends and wrote many lovely songs for them. He was often to be found on his hands and knees at home with several of the youngest children on his back! He used to let them accompany him on his long hikes over the mountains, and to the swimming pools. Oftentimes the younger children would fall asleep on his knee, and it is said that on one such occasion, he found the inspiration for his lovely "Cradle Song" or "Lullaby," and had completely finished it in his mind before he wrote the manuscript.

Chaliapin, Feodor (1873)

Feodor Chaliapin, the famous basso, was once invited to attend a dinner in honor of the late world famous tenor, Enrico Caruso. Toasts were given in honor of Caruso but Chaliapin, equally famous, was ignored. Finally, unable to stand the slight any longer, he rose after being called upon to say a few words and remarked, "Gentlemen, every morning the orthodox Arabs, while saying their prayers, thank Allah that they were born men and not women. I, too, say my prayers every morning, and thank God that I was born a basso and not a tenor."

Chopin, Frederic F. (1810–1849)

In the early years of his life, Chopin was considered a great pianist, but not much as a composer. He finally published a set of variations for the piano, and Schumann, at the time editor of a musical journal, commented on the compositions, concluding his article, "Hats off, gentlemen, a genius." One day many years later, Chopin was browsing through the imperial library in Vienna, and came across a small volume with the name Chopin as author. Not knowing any other Chopin, his curiosity led him to glance inside the volume and was surprised to find music in his own handwriting. The publisher of the variations had also recognized his genius and had sent a copy to the library of the emperor!

Chopin's father was a boarding-school master and had under his charge a number of very unruly boys. No one was able to control them until one day young Chopin gathered the boys around him and announced that he would tell them a story. He told them a story of robbers and robbers' caves, all the while playing a soft piano accompaniment. As he told them how the robbers, tired after a strenuous day had fallen asleep in the woods, the music he played, which was not written but improvised from melodies in his mind, had such an effect on the boys that they fell asleep one by one. Chopin often used this incident in his later life to illustrate the power of music.

Debussy, Claude Achille (1862–1918)

Debussy found the inspiration for many of his children's compositions while watching his beloved little daughter play. For example, she possessed a doll which she called "Golliwog." She made it stand and walk, and the peculiar actions of the doll were so like the dance the negroes called the cakewalk, that Debussy sat down and wrote a composition which he called the "Golliwog's Cakewalk."

DePachmann, Vladimir (1848)

DePachmann and Godowsky, both great pianists, were also great friends. Some years ago friends of DePachmann arranged a dinner in his honor. He attended, accompanied by Godowsky. The guest of honor carefully checked each item of the service and exclaimed, "Everything is of the best, as it should be for the great DePachmann." The dinner commenced. As each course was served, DePachmann exchanged dishes with Godowsky until the latter irritatedly asked him for an explanation. DePachmann with a twinkle in his eye said, "Because, my dear friend, the waiter looks like one of Paderewski's patriots, and how do I know he isn't trying to poison me?" Having fun at each other's expense is one of the most frequent and one of the most lovable traits of the great musicians.

DePachmann received one day a note from Godowsky, asking him to take as a pupil a young friend of his. This friend, he said, was very modest, and asked that DePachmann treat him generously. The word "modest" annoyed DePachmann who flew into a rage, greatly embarrassing the young man who had brought the note and who turned out to be the young man in question. Finally DePachmann turned to the young man and asked him to play for him. Owing to his modesty and to the great man's tantrums, the young man made a poor showing. After he had gone DePachmann exclaimed, "Humph! Modesty! I am not modest yet, and he is already modest. The impudence!"

Foster, Stephen Collins (1826–1864)

When Stephen Collins Foster, beloved writer of American folk songs, was a young man, he became very fond of Jane McDowell, daughter of a physician. While calling at the McDowell home young Stephen became acquainted with Joe, the negro butler. He became quite fond of Joe, and on one occasion promised to "write him in a song." Later, remembering his lightly undertaken obligation, he wrote "Old Black Joe," which has been a universal favorite ever since.

Gluck, Christophe Willibald (1714–1787)

Gluck was writing his opera "Iphigenia in Aulis," when Vestria, one of Europe's greatest dancers asked him to include in the opera a chaconne, a dance of Spanish origin, for Vestria's son to dance. "No," said Gluck, "this is a Greek opera and the Greeks knew nothing of the chaconne." Vestria insisted, however, and said, "You must write a chaconne for my son to dance. I am the god of the dance." Greatly angered, Gluck said, "Go dance in heaven then, and leave my opera alone." However, it is interesting to note that in order to keep everyone happy, Gluck did write the chaconne, which explains why a Spanish dance is found in a Greek opera.

Grieg, Edvard Hagrup (1843–1907)

An amusing story is told of Edvard Grieg, the famous Norwegian composer. As a boy, he detested going to school. One day, after going to school in the rain, he was sent home to dry his clothes. This gave him an idea. The next time it rained, he made it a point to get wet, and was sent home again. Then came a long spell of dry weather, and finally another day came when it started to sprinkle, and Edvard, afraid he would not be sufficiently wet to be sent home, stopped at a pump and wet his clothes. This time, however, it didn't work, because by the time he got to school, the sun was shining and the teacher merely made him sit in the sunshine.

Handel, Georg Friedrich (1685–1759)

A revealing story is told of the wit of the great Handel, who owned the Opera house in London and played the harpsichord in the orchestra, directing the orchestra at the same time. He was such a fine player on this instrument that he oftentimes attracted more attention from the audience than did the opera singers. This so infuriated one of the Italian singers, that he threatened Handel, adding that if it happened again, he would jump down on Handel's harpsichord. Handel replied, "Oh you will, will you? Well, just let me know the day before you expect to do it, and I'll advertise it in the paper and we will have a great many more people here to see it than come to hear you sing!"

Sometimes the will to learn music in the mind of him who loves it proves so strong that almost any obstacle in the way is overcome. Handel as a boy was very fond of music; his father wanted him to become a great lawyer. With the help of an aunt who was very kind to him, little George smuggled an old, battered harpsichord into the attic of the Handel home one day when the family was out. Late at night the young boy would steal to the attic and play very softly on the instrument. One night he forgot himself and began to play more loudly than usual, with the result that the family, upon investigating, were greeted by the somewhat strange picture of a young lad clad only in nightgown and cap playing original tunes in an attic. After this the father was not so averse to his son's interest in music, with the result that Handel became one of the greatest composers of all time.

Handel composed his greatest work, the "Messiah" in twenty-one days. It was dedicated to the Irish people, and he was asked to present it when it was completed, in Dublin. A day of celebration was declared, and even the doors of the debtor's prison were opened in order that all might hear the wonderful music. Ladies expecting to attend were asked not to wear hoop skirts in order that the crowd be accommodated. The performance was given for charity, and was one of the greatest events in the great composer's life. Students at the university were so enthusiastic that they insisted on drawing his carriage. Returning to England, Handel was received with the greatest acclaim ever accorded a musician. He again performed the Messiah, and the audience was moved to such an extent that they rose to their feet at the singing of the great "Hallelujah Chorus." Since then it has been customary for audiences in England and America to rise during the singing of this great chorus.

Several stories are told of Handel's terrible temper. He once engaged the great singer Cuzzane, for the first performance of his opera "Ottone." Being temperamental, the singer failed to arrive until the rehearsals were well under way. When she did arrive, she refused to sing the aria according to Handel's direction. Handel flew into a rage and threatened to throw her out the window unless she obeyed. Frightened out of her wits, the singer followed his direction and gave one of the outstanding performances of her career. On another occasion Handel became enraged at the concertmeister in his orchestra. Handel snatched the violinist's instrument out of his hands and smashed it over his head. It happened to be a genuine Stradivarius and this act of temper cost Handel a great deal of money. At another time, Handel so angered Matheson during Handel's conducting of one of his operas, that a duel was fought. During the duel, Handel's life was saved when Matheson's rapier struck a button and was deflected as it was about to enter his heart.

Haydn, Franz Josef (1732–1809)

Franz Haydn once applied to Reutter, the great choirmaster, for a position as a choirboy. Reutter was somewhat abrupt, and gruffly asked Haydn if he could trill. Haydn spoke up and said that Reutter himself could not trill. So Reutter told him to attend him carefully while he showed Haydn how. Haydn gave so perfect an imitation of the master's trill that Reutter delightedly gave him a coin.

An interesting story is told of Haydn's boyhood. When he was six years old, he was sent to his cousin, a successful choirmaster, to be trained in the choir. There was to be a great celebration in Hamburg, and everything seemed to be in readiness when suddenly the drummer who was to play in the procession became violently ill. Young Haydn's cousin knew not what to do. He remembered how well Haydn had kept time with two sticks of wood while at home, so he immediately showed the young boy how to hold the drumsticks and left him to practice. Young Haydn quickly stretched a piece of cloth over a meal barrel and set to work. The meal flew in all directions. Imagine the surprise of the choirmaster, upon returning home, and finding his young pupil on the floor playing the makeshift drum with great gusto, but all covered with meal. However, the young lad had so thoroughly mastered the difficulties of drumming that his playing in the procession later had all the earmarks of a professional. Too, the sight of such a diminutive player proved a great source of merriment and wonder to the onlookers at the parade.

A pathetic incident is related in the life of Haydn. Although his father was very poor, he managed to send Haydn to school in Vienna. Haydn, however, had to depend for his living on his salary as a choirboy. One day, one of the other boys played a boyish prank, so infuriating Haydn that he snatched a pair of shears and snipped off the other boy's pigtail. For this he was dismissed from school. He wandered the streets for a time without food and finally was noticed by a young acquaintance who remarked about his starved appearance. The young man took him home with him to share his room and what food he could procure. Haydn worked so industriously that before long he was able to repay his friend.

Haydn was a very particular man. Everything about his well ordered life had to be exact in every detail. Frederic II once presented him with a diamond ring. Before Haydn would sit down at the piano to compose, he insisted on having the ring on his finger, his wig properly powdered, and dressed carefully in his best suit. Then and not until then, would he attempt to write a composition. He said, "I can't compose unless I am in the mood; I can't get in the proper mood unless everything is just so; then I cast about for a theme and write."

When the University of Oxford honored Haydn with a Doctor's degree, he was expected to write a composition and submit it to the committee of professors. One day, the professors received a few lines from Haydn inclosing a few measures of music. The music was so short that they were offended, and called the committee together to discuss the matter. Upon closer observation they discovered that the composition was a perfect melody capable of being played backwards, forwards, or upside down. No matter which way it was played it was the same composition. The committee agreed unanimously that Haydn had once more shown evidence of his great genius.

Hubay, Jeno (1858)

Jeno Hubay was interested in composition when but a boy. His father, however, being a musician, decided that another profession would be better for the boy. So Jeno began studying architecture. But he loved to compose in his spare time and at the age of eleven entered a composition in a contest for which his father was judge. While his father was playing the composition Jeno's heart was in his mouth. Finally his father said, "I'd like to know who wrote that. He's an ass, and doesn't know anything, but he has talent."

Josquin, (Josquin Des Pres) (1450–1521)

Several centuries ago, the famous Flemish composer Josquin was appointed choirmaster in the chapel of the king of France. One of the promises made Josquin was in the matter of money, but King Louis forgot all about that part of it, and caused Josquin much distress. In fact he was barely able to live. Finally he hit upon an idea. Part of the 119th Psalm reads, "O think of thy servant as concerning Thy word." Josquin composed a motet with these words as the theme, and played it for the king in the chapel service. King Louis was not only struck by the music, but remembered his promise, and began paying Josquin's salary.

Lablache, Luigi (1794–1858)

The great basso of the past century, Luigi Lablache, was once called upon to sing for the king. While waiting in the anteroom for the audition, he was so nervous that he forgot to remove his hat. On being called, he unconsciously picked up another hat, and with his own on his head, and another in his hand, marched in to see the king. The king with customary humor, and a twinkle in his eye, said, "Pray tell me which of the two hats is your own, the one in your hand or the one on your head. Or did you bring two in case you should leave one behind?" Lablache was struck by one of his sudden witty ideas. "Ah!" he cried, "two hats are indeed too many for a man who has no head at all."

Lehmann, Lilli (1848–1929)

Occasionally an obscure artist becomes famous because of the illness of someone else. Lilli Lehmann was long ago appearing in one of the minor roles of Mozart's "The Magic Flute." After a run of two weeks the prima donna was suddenly stricken, and Lilli went on the stage in the prima donna's role, although she had never studied it, depending solely on her memory, having heard the role sung so many times. Suffice it to say that henceforth the star of Lilli Lehmann was ever in the ascendancy.

MacDowell, Edward (1861–1908)

Edward MacDowell, America's great composer, as a small boy disliked practicing his piano lessons. One day he became entranced in a story book and bribed his brother to make a noise on the piano while he finished his book. This might have worked out had not a visitor called and asked to hear Edward play. As a consequence the ruse was discovered and Edward had to do two hours practice instead of one.

MacDowell taught for a time in Europe. Marian Nevins went to Europe to study and was sent to MacDowell for lessons. He held a low opinion of American girls as music students, but after protest, was persuaded to accept her as a pupil. A short time later he was in turn accepted as her husband.

It is said that MacDowell was his own severest critic. He would throw sheet after sheet of manuscript into the wastebasket, sometimes abandoning a composition entirely and starting something else. The story is told that MacDowell's wife was emptying the wastebasket one day, and paused to look at some of the work that had been thrown away. One of the scraps of manuscript impressed her as being too worthy a piece to discard, and she saved it. The composition was eventually published, and today is probably MacDowell's best known piano piece. Its title is "To a Wild Rose."

Marcello, Benedetto (1686–1739)

The story is told of Benedetto Marcello, who was very superstitious, that on the way to mass he slipped on a stone, and fell into an old tomb. The shock was very great, and the accident was interpreted by him as a foreboding of death. He changed his whole order of life and dedicated himself to his work.

Mendelssohn, Felix (1809–1847)

Felix Mendelssohn as a lad of eleven had the rare opportunity of visiting with the famous poet Goethe. Goethe was very fond of the music of Bach, and asked Mendelssohn to play one of Bach's compositions which had especially attracted his interest and attention. Mendelssohn did not have the music, but sat down at the piano and started playing. About half way through the composition he had forgotten the melody. He went right on improvising, however, and Goethe never knew that the music young Felix was playing was not Bach's but Mendelssohn's own.

Mendelssohn, although a German, was very popular in England. He made a number of journeys to London and became quite friendly with the king and queen. On one occasion he called at the royal household, and while there was asked by Queen Victoria to play. He sat down at the piano, which was dusty, and the queen got a dustcloth and cleaned it for him. He sang to her in English, and she, to return the compliment, sang a little song to him in German. He later wrote to his sister Fanny, "The Queen has a charming voice, and needs only a little cultivation and practice to make her fit to take a leading part in Elijah."

Much wonder has been caused by the addition of the name Bartholdy to that of Felix Mendelssohn in many of his compositions. Felix' family was Jewish, although Felix and the other children had been baptized as Lutherans. Felix' grandfather had done a great deal of work in helping the Jews in the Ghetto, and was, as a consequence greatly revered by them. Felix began to win fame as a composer at an early age, and his father, fearful that his popularity would detract from his grandfather's insisted that he add his mother's maiden name to his compositions. Since that time his compositions have all been signed "Felix Mendelssohn-Bartholdy."

Mozart, Wolfgang Amadeus (1756–1791)

The boyhood history of Mozart is probably more interesting than that of any other composer. He was the world's most famous musical child prodigy. He used to listen to his father give piano lessons to his sister, and after the lesson he could play the exercises from memory. This was at the age of three! By the time he was five he had done a great deal of composing, and by the time he was ten he was an expert player on the clavier, and read the most difficult music at sight. The Austrian emperor heard about young Mozart and sent for him to discover for himself whether the rumors of his talent were true. Mozart played for him and the emperor was, of course, convinced. One day as a joke, he asked Mozart to play the organ with the keys covered. His surprise was complete, when the lad covered the keyboard with a sheet and played just as sweetly as before.

When only six years of age Mozart was composing music. His father would help him by writing down the notes as the son played the music on the harpsichord. One day when his father was away, young Mozart attempted to write down the notes of his new composition for himself. His father came home and found him busily engaged with pen and paper. He asked his son what he was writing, and the child replied, "A concerto for the harpsichord." The elder Mozart picked up the ink-smeared paper to see what his son had written, but could not make out the notes at first. Gradually he was able to get at the meaning of the strange markings, and was greatly surprised at the matureness of the work. "But this is too difficult to play," he exclaimed. The boy said, "One must practice it until he can play it. Listen, I'll play this part for you." He went to the harpsichord and tried to play what he had written. He knew how every note should be played, but his little fingers could not execute the difficult passage. Mozart composed his first symphony when only seven years of age, and had also learned to play the violin.

Mozart was well known for his ability to work speedily. Many of his compositions were written in a great hurry, although they were accurately done. When he was producing one of his finest operas, "Don Giovanni," he had not written the overture until the last night of the rehearsals. The last rehearsal was not over until after midnight and when Mozart reached home he was so tired he lay down for a short rest, asking his wife to wake him in a short time. He was sleeping so soundly, however, that his wife could not bear to waken him, and he slept until five o'clock. Waking suddenly in alarm, he rushed to his desk and wrote the great overture to "Don Giovanni" in two hours. It was ready for the copiers who arrived at seven, but the orchestra had to play it without a rehearsal.

Allegri's "Miserere" was a composition so prized that it was never performed outside the Sistine Chapel. The singers could not even take the music home for practice. Mozart had long wanted to hear the composition, and journeyed to Rome to hear its annual presentation. It made such an impression on him that he went home and wrote the entire composition from memory. He was only fourteen at the time, and this achievement caused a great stir among the musicians of the day.

Pons, Lily (1905)

Lily Pons' remarkable success as a singer has been as great a surprise to her as to the public. She graduated from the Paris Conservatory with a major in piano at the age of thirteen. Before she had ever had a chance to sing in public, a scout from the Metropolitan Opera Company engaged her to appear in New York. She arrived in March, 1930, and a short time later had been awarded three contracts, one for work at the Metropolitan for five years, one for phonograph records, and one for a series of public concerts. When someone told her that she had "plucked three plums from the tree of good fortune" she cried, "No, zey fall on my head."

Rossini, Gioachino (1792–1868)

Rossini had a great deal of difficulty in remembering the names of people he met. After being introduced to the composer Bishop, and meeting again the next day, he remembered his face but could not recall the name. Considerably embarrassed, he said, "Ah, my dear Mr. er—;" and then he had an idea. To show Bishop he had not really forgotten him, he whistled Bishop's composition, "When the Wind Blows," which was considered by Bishop a great compliment.

Schubert, Franz Peter (1797–1828)

While climbing in the mountains near Vienna, Franz Schubert one day stopped at an inn for rest. He noticed a group of gaily dressed people standing gloomily about. The innkeeper explained that the group comprised a bridal party and that there was no music for dancing. So Schubert sat down at the ancient piano, and played for hours while the party danced.

As was so frequently the case, Schubert one day met some of his literary friends in a popular cafe. One of them was thumbing through a volume of Shakespeare. Schubert picked up the volume a bit later, and by chance opened to the lines of "Hark, Hark, the Lark" in the drama, "Cymbeline." The beauty of the words struck him with tremendous force, and he snatched a bill of fare and immediately began to set the words to music. In a few moments one of the finest examples of the art song was given to posterity.

Schubert was in the habit of jotting down melodies at once whenever they came to his mind. He would often lie awake at night trying to think of themes for new songs. When an inspiration came to him he would bound out of bed and write down the music at once. So fearful was he that the new phrases might escape his memory that he wore his glasses while he slept, so that valuable moments would not be wasted in putting them on when he wished to write.

Schumann, Robert (1810–1856)

Robert Schumann developed his musical talent later in life than most of the famous composers. His parents wanted him to be an author or a poet, but he finally decided that his love of music was too strong to allow him to consider any other profession seriously. He did not give up his interest in other things, however, and we find him in later years editor of one of the foremost musical journals of Europe. His ambition was enormous, and not satisfied with being just a good pianist, he wanted to become the greatest. Therefore he set about making his technique better than that of the other musicians. His first attempt was to make his fingers work better than other pianist's fingers, and in using a mechanical device to strengthen the little finger of his right hand, he so weakened it that he had to give up his playing. So he turned to composing, and it is quite possible that had this accident not occurred, we might have missed the beautiful music which he later composed.

Wagner, Richard (1813–1883)

Many of the great composers were also great men in other fields. Most of them were, to some extent at least, philosophers. Reading their letters gives us a much clearer insight into the more personal side of their lives. Richard Wagner, for example, during the first part of his life as a composer, was very unhappy. Financial troubles, lack of recognition, and many disappointments caused him on one occasion to write to Liszt, his great friend, "Dear Franz: None of the past years have gone by without having at least once driven me to the verge of suicide." Liszt, sympathetic and understanding soul that he was, wrote, "Your letters are sad and your life sadder still. You want to go out into the wide world, live, enjoy, revel! Ah! how cordially I wish you could. But your greatness constitutes also your misery—and the two are inseparably united and must ever annoy and torture you." Liszt was aware of the fact that in order to create great music, one must know joys and sorrows, tragedy, and pain, for these are the bases of emotion.

Wagner was a very serious student and quite capable in many lines of endeavor. He was especially interested in the Greek classics. In fact his interest was so pronounced that he translated the first twelve books of the Odyssey. His study of Greek mythology led him to writing plays, all of them tragedies. Working for two years on a play in which all of the forty-two characters were killed, he had to revive them as ghosts in order to complete the ending.

Ysaye, Eugene (1858–1931)

Eugene Ysaye, the great violinist, made a tour of the west, and tells an interesting story of his appearance in a Montana town. He was using a chaconne by Bach for the first time on a concert stage, and found everyone eager to hear it. While seated at dinner, a burly westerner came to his table and gave his name and asked how much he would charge to play the chaconne for him. Ysaye refused to consider it, but the westerner would not take no for an answer. He offered five hundred dollars, a thousand dollars, and finally pulled out a roll of bills and a gun and said, "Play." Needless to say, Ysaye played!

SELECTED REFERENCES

Miscellaneous

DICKINSON, EDWARD, *The Education of a Music Lover.* C. Scribner's Sons, 1911.

Encyclopedia of Music and Musicians, Macmillan.

ERB, JOHN LAWRENCE, *Music Appreciation for the Student.* G. Schirmer, Inc., 1926.

ERSKINE, *A Musical Companion.* Knopf, 1935.

HAMILTON, C. G., *Music Appreciation.* Oliver Ditson Co.; C. H. Ditson & Co., 1920.

MATHEWS, W. S. B., *How to Understand Music.* Theodore Presser Company, 1904.

SPAETH, SIGMUND, *The Art of Enjoying Music.* Whittlesby House McGraw Hill Book Company, Inc., 1933.

SPAETH, SIGMUND, *Great Symphonies.* Garden City Pub. Co.

CHAPTER I

Musical Theory

ANDERSON, A. O., *Musical Theory.* H. T. FitzSimons, 1926.

BERNSTEIN, MARTIN, *Introduction to Music.* Prentice-Hall, Inc., 1937.

BORLAND, J. E., *Musical Foundations.* Carl Fischer, Inc., 1927.

ELSON, ARTHUR, *The Book of Musical Knowledge.* Houghton Mifflin Co., 1927.

ELSON, L. C., *Elson's Music Dictionary.* Oliver Ditson Company, 1905.

GARDNER, C. E., *Essentials of Music Theory.* Carl Fischer, Inc., 1912.

GEHRKENS, K. W., *Music Notation and Terminology.* A. S. Barnes Company, 1918.

JONES, R. G., *Theory of Music.* Harper and Brothers, 1936.

SMITH, M., and KRONE, M. T. *Fundamentals of Musicianship.* Witmark and Sons, 1934.

CHAPTER II

Harmony

FOOTE AND SPALDING, *Modern Harmony.* A. P. Schmidt Company, 1924.

GIST, *Keyboard Harmony for Juniors.* Oliver Ditson.

GOETSCHIUS, PERCY, *The Theory and Practice of Tone Relations.* G. Schirmer, Inc., 1900.

HEACOX, A. E., *Harmony for Ear, Eye and Keyboard.* Oliver Ditson Company.

OREM, *Students Harmony Book.* Clayton F. Summy Co.

TAPPER, THOMAS, *First Year Harmony.* A. P. Schmidt Company, 1908.

CHAPTER III

History of Music

BALTZELL, W. J., *A Complete History of Music.* Theodore Presser Co., 1905.

BAUER, HEINRICH, *Practical History of the Violin.* H. Bauer Music Co., 1911.

BAUER, MARION, *Twentieth Century Music.* G. P. Putnam's Sons, 1933.

BAUER, MARION, and PEYSER, ETHEL, *How Music Grew.* G. P. Putnam's Sons, 1925.

BAUER, MARION, and PEYSER, ETHEL, *Music Through the Ages.* G. P. Putnam's Sons, 1932.

BEKKER, PAUL, *The Story of Music.* W. W. Norton and Company, Inc., 1927.

COOKE, J. F., *Standard History of Music.* Theodore Presser Co., 1910.

FERGUSON, D. S., *History of Musical Thought.* Crofts and Co., 1936.

GANTVOORT, A. J. *Familiar Talks on the History of Music.* G. Schirmer, 1919.

GROVE, SIR GEORGE, *Grove's Dictionary of Music and Musicians.* The Macmillan Company, 1904-1910-1920.

HAMILTON, C. G., *Outlines of Musical History.* Oliver Ditson Company, 1908.

HENDERSON, W. J., *The Story of Music.* Longmans Green, and Company, 1912.

KINSCELLA, H. G., *Music and Romance.* RCA Victor Company, 1930.

MCGEHEE, T. C., *People and Music.* Allyn and Bacon, 1929.

MASON, D. G., *From Song to Symphony.* Oliver Ditson Company, 1924.

PRATT, W. S., *The History of Music.* 4th ed. 1911.

UPTON, G. P., *The Standard Operas: their plots and their music.* A. C. McClurg and Co., 1928.

CHAPTER IV

Musical Form

FAULKNER, A. S., *What We Hear in Music.* RCA Victor Corporation, 1929.

GOETSCHIUS, PERCY, *The Material Used in Musical Composition.* G. Schirmer.

GOETSCHIUS, PERCY, *Lessons in Music Form.* Oliver Ditson Company; C. H. Ditson and Co., 1904.

GOODRICH, A. J., *Musical Analysis.* The John Church Company, 1914.

PAUER, ERNST, *Musical Forms.* Novello, Ewer and Co.; Oliver Ditson & Co., 1878.

TAPPER, THOMAS, *First Year Analysis.* A. P. Schmidt Company, 1914.

CHAPTER V

Musical Instruments

CAIN, N. *Choral Music and Its Practice.* M. Witmark and Sons.

COWARD, SIR HENRY, *Choral Technique and Interpretation.* H. W. Gray Co., 1914.

FORSYTH, CECIL, *Orchestration.* Macmillan & Co., Ltd., 1914.

MASON, DANIEL G., *The Orchestral Instruments and What They Do.* Gray, 1909.

MILLS, WESLEY, *Voice Production in Singing and Speaking.* J. B. Lippincott Co., 1913.

RIMSKY-KORSAKOW, *Principles of Orchestration.* Kalmus.

SCHWARTZ, HARRY WAYNE, *The Story of Musical Instruments.* Doubleday, 1938.

CHAPTER VI

Brief Biographies of Great Composers

BAKER, THEODORE, *A Biographical Dictionary of Musicians.* G. Schirmer, 1905.

EWEN, DAVID, *Composers of Today.* H. W. Wilson and Co., 1934.

MASON, D. G., *Contemporary Composers.* The Macmillan Company, 1918.

MASON, D. G., *The Romantic Composers.* The Macmillan Company, 1906.

NEWMAN, ERNEST, *The Life of Richard Wagner.* A. A. Knopf, 1933.

NEWMAN, ERNEST, *The Unconscious Beethoven.* A. A. Knopf, 1927.

REIS, CLAIRE RAPHAEL, *Composers in America.* The Macmillan Company, 1937.

ROLLAND, ROMAIN, *Beethoven the Creator.* Harper & Brothers, 1929.

SCHOLES-EARHART, *The Complete Book of Great Musicians.* Oxford.

SPECHT, RICHARD, *Beethoven as He Lived.* H. Smith and R. Haas, 1933.

CHAPTER VII

Musical Anecdotes

NUSSBAUM, MRS. F. *Mirth, Music, and Memory.* Bruce Humphries, Inc., 1937.

SPAETH, SIGMUND, *Stories Behind the World's Great Music.* McGraw Hill, 1937.

GLOSSARY OF MUSICAL TERMS

A Cappella — Vocal music without accompaniment.
A Tempo — In time. Usually a return to the original tempo.
Accelerando — (*accel.*) Gradually faster.
Accent — Stress or emphasis.
Accidental — A sharp, flat, or natural sign placed before a note to change its pitch.
Adagio — A slow tempo, slower than Andante, not so slow as Lento.
Air — The melody, or tune.
Allegretto — A moderately fast tempo, faster than Moderato, slower than Allegro.
Allegro — A quick, lively tempo, faster than Moderato, slower than Vivace.
Alto — The lowest of the women's voices. Also Contralto.
Andante — A moderately slow tempo, faster than Adagio, slower than Moderato.
Andantino — Slightly faster than Andante.
Animato — Animated, lively.
Anthem — A religious choral composition.
Arco — With the bow.
Aria — A solo vocal form, part of an opera or oratorio.
Arpeggio — A broken chord, distinguished from a simultaneous chord.
Art Song — An artistic song in which the music closely fits the words.
Augmented — A term applied to major and perfect intervals enlarged by one-half step.

Ballad — A narrative song.
Ballet — An artistic group dance, usually expressing a story in pantomime.
Barcarolle — A boat song, usually having a smoothly flowing melody.
Baritone — A male voice, between tenor and bass in pitch. Also an instrument.
Bass — The lowest male voice. Also an instrument.
Berceuse — A lullaby, or cradle song.
Binary — A two-part song form.
Bridge — A support for the strings of stringed instruments.

Cadence — A harmonic ending.
Cantata — A composition with choral and solo parts, built around a central theme.
Carol — A festal folk-song, usually on a Christmas or Easter theme.
Chaconne — A dance-like form, of Spanish origin.
Chamber music — Music for a small group intended for a small room.
Chant — A religious song, with groups of words sung on the same pitch.
Choir — A group of singers, usually for a church service.
Chorale — A hymn-like type of music, usually sacred.
Chord — Three or more tones sounded together harmonically.
Chromatic — Progressing by half-tone intervals.
Classic — Music written with adherence to a strict pattern or form.
Coda — An extended ending of a composition.
Coloratura — A specialized type of high soprano voice.
Composer — One who writes music.
Composition — A piece of music; the art of writing music.
Con — An Italian prefix meaning "with."
Concert — A public musical performance.
Concerto — A composition for solo instrument with orchestral accompaniment.
Con fuoco — With fire.
Con moto — With motion.
Consonance — A chord or combination of sounds pleasing to the ear. Opposed to dissonance.
Con sordino — With mute. (Applies only to stringed instruments.)
Contralto — The lowest woman's voice. Also alto.
Contrapuntal — Relating to counterpoint.

Counterpoint — The setting of one melody against another.
Crescendo — (*cresc.*) Increasing in loudness.

Da Capo — (*D. C.*) To the beginning.
Dal Segno — (*D. S.*) Literally, from the sign.
Decrescendo — (*decresc.*) Decreasing in loudness.
Diatonic — Progressing by scale intervals.
Diminished — A term applied to minor and perfect intervals made smaller by one-half step.
Diminuendo — (*dim.*) Gradually softer.
Dissonance — A combination of sounds unsatisfying to the ear. Opposed to consonance.
Duet — A song for two solo voices or instruments.

Embouchure — Tongue and lip control in instrumental tone-production.
Ensemble — Together; a group of players playing together.
Etude — A musical study or exercise.

Fantasia — A free and fanciful form of composition.
Finale — The last part, or close of a composition.
Fine — A term indicating the termination of a composition.
Flat — A symbol (♭) indicating that a tone is to be lowered in pitch one-half step.
Folk-song — A song characteristic of a people or nation.
Forte — (*f*) Loud.
Fortissimo — (*ff*) Very loud.
Forzando — (*sf*) Strongly accented. The same as sforzando (*sfz*).
Fugue — A common form of contrapuntal composition.
Fundamental — A term applied to the lowest note of a chord in normal position.

Gavotte — A dance form.
Glee — A choral composition for three or four voices.
Grave — A slow and solemn movement. The slowest tempo in music.

Harmonics — Overtones obtained on instruments or voice; usually applied to stringed instruments.
Harmony — Combinations of tones into chords and chordal progressions.
Hexachord — A scale or system of six tones.
Hymn — A common form of religious song, intended to be sung by the congregation.

Intermezzo — An instrumental interlude.
Interval — The distance between two tones.
Intonation — The act of production of tone in exact tune or pitch.
Invention — A short composition in free contrapuntal style.
Inversion — A change in position from the normal of an interval or chord.

Key — A system of tone relationships following the pattern of a recognized scale.

Largo — A very slow tempo.
Legato — Connected.
Lento — A slow tempo, slower than Adagio, faster than Largo.
Libretto — The text or words of an opera or oratorio.

Madrigal — A secular part song developed during the sixteenth century.
Maestoso — Majestically.
Major — Greater, when referring to intervals or scales. Opposed to minor.
Marcato — Marked; accented.
March — A military air or composition.
Mass — A choral composition performed at the celebration of High Mass.
Mazurka — A dance form of Polish origin.
Measure — The space between two bar lines on the staff.
Melody — A pleasing succession of tones, usually having a pleasing rhythm.
Meno — Less.
Meno mosso — Less motion; slower.
Mezzo-forte — (*mf*) Medium loud.

Mezzo-piano — (*mp*) medium soft.
Minor — Less, when referring to intervals or scales. Opposed to major.
Minuet — A dance form. The court dance of France in the 18th and 19th centuries.
Modes — Kinds of scale patterns, as minor and major modes.
Moderato — A moderate, average tempo.
Modulation — The process of moving harmonically to a different key.
Monody — For one voice, as opposed to polyphony.
Morendo — Dying away; gradually diminishing the tone and the tempo.
Motet — A sacred choral composition, usually in contrapuntal style.
Muted — Softened, by means of a mute.

Natural — A symbol (♮) used to cancel the effect of a sharp or a flat.
Neumes — A type of notes used in the middle ages.
Nocturne — A night song.
Notation — The representation of tones by written or printed characters.

Obbligato — An instrumental part usually accompanying a vocal solo.
Octet — A composition for eight voices or instruments.
Opera — A musical drama.
Opera comique — Comic opera.
Operetta — A light musical drama with spoken dialogue.
Opus — Literally, a "work." A musical composition or group of compositions.
Oratorio — A sacred musical drama in concert form.
Overtones — Complementary harmonic sounds present in all musical tones.
Overture — An introductory part to an opera or oratorio; a musical form sometimes a separate form.

Passion — A sacred composition depicting the suffering of Christ.
Pastorale — A musical picture of scenes from rural life.
Pentatonic — Five-tone.
Percussion — Referring to instruments which are played by striking.
Piano — (*p*) Soft. Also the pianoforte.
Pianissimo — (*pp*) Very soft.
Pitch — The rate of vibration of any given tone.
Piu — More.
Piu Mosso — More motion; quicker.
Plainsong — The name given to the earliest form of religious chant.
Pizzicato — (*pizz.*) Plucking. Opposed to *arco* (bowing).
Poco a poco — Little by little.
Polka — A dance form of Bohemian origin.
Polonaise — A Polish dance form.
Polyphonic — Many-voiced. Opposed to monophonic.
Prelude — Introductory movement of a composition. A musical form.
Prestissimo — As fast as possible.
Presto — Very fast.
Prima donna — A principal woman singer in opera.
Program (music) — Descriptive music. Opposed to absolute or pure music.

Quartet — A composition written for four voices or instruments.
Quintet — A composition written for five voices or instruments.

Rallentando — (*rall.*) Gradually slower.
Recitative — Musical declamation usually introducing an aria.
Recital — A form of musical program usually by one artist.
Repertory — A list of compositions which any artist has ready for performance.
Rhapsody — An instrumental fantasia usually based on national melodies.
Rhythm — A periodic recurrence of accent; regular pulsation.
Ritard — (*rit.*) Slower.
Romantic — Referring to the period in music between the classic and modern.

Rondo — A musical form wherein a principal theme recurs several times.
Round — A short song in two or more parts sung at different time intervals.
Rubato — Robbed time. Time taken from one note and given to another.

Scale — The succession of tones upon which music is built.
Scherzo — A piece of a lively, sportive character.
Schottische — A dance form in rather slow tempo.
Score — The musical notation of a composition. The conductor's score.
Secular — Worldly, as opposed to religious.
Semitone — Half-tone.
Senza — Without.
Septet — A composition written for seven voices or instruments.
Serenade — A nocturnal love song.
Sextet — A composition written for six voices or instruments.
Sharp — A symbol (♯) used to raise a tone one-half step in pitch.
Signature — A group of sharps or flats indicating the key of a composition. Figures indicating the meter of a composition.
Slur — Passing smoothly from one tone to another without break.
Solmization — The practice of applying syllable names to scale tones.
Solo — A composition for one voice or instrument.
Sonata — An extensive instrumental composition, of three or four movements.
Soprano — The highest female voice.
Sordino — A mute.
Sostenuto — Sustained.
Spiritual — A type of religious folk-song peculiar to the American Negro.
Staccato — Detached; Notes played sharply separated from each other. Indicated by dots (...) over notes.
Staff — The five parallel horizontal lines on which musical notes are written.
Strain — A portion of a composition, separated by a double bar. A period.
Stringendo — Faster.
Suite — A series of short related compositions under one title.
Symphonic Poem — An extensive orchestral work usually in one movement.
Symphony — A composition of several movements for full orchestra, based on the sonata form.
Syncopate — To place the accent on an unconventional beat.

Tacet — Silent.
Tango — A dance form originating in Argentina.
Tenor — The highest male voice.
Tenuto — Held. Sustained for full time value.
Ternary — A three part song form.
Tetrachord — A group of four notes, the basis of the Greek scale system.
Theme — A musical subject. Contrasted with *development*.
Toccata — An old form of composition for organ requiring great technique.
Tone — A musical sound of definite pitch.
Transposition — The process of performing in another than the written key.
Treble — The upper part; the highest voice.
Tremolo — A trembling or quivering. A shaking of the tone.
Triad — The common chord, consisting of a root, third, and fifth.
Trio — A composition for three voices or instruments.
Tutti — All; used after a solo passage to mean all instruments or voices.

Unison — Two or more tones having the same pitch.

Vibrato — A tremulous effect, akin to tremolo but less marked.
Virtuoso — An accomplished artist.
Vivace — Lively, briskly.
Vivo — Animated, lively.

Waltz — A dance form, of German origin.

INDEX